THE *Butterfly* BLUEPRINT

REVITALIZE YOUR RELATIONSHIP AND KEEP YOUR HEART FLUTTERING FOREVER

AMANDA GREEN MSW, RSW

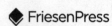 FriesenPress

One Printers Way
Altona, MB R0G 0B0
Canada

www.friesenpress.com

ISBN
978-1-03-830052-2 (Hardcover)
978-1-03-830051-5 (Paperback)
978-1-03-830053-9 (eBook)

1. FAMILY & RELATIONSHIPS, LOVE & ROMANCE

Distributed to the trade by The Ingram Book Company

Disclaimer

All of the couples described in this book are fictional or composites of multiple real-life scenarios. The narratives have been crafted to provide insights and guidance for various relationship dynamics and do not represent any specific individuals or relationships. The names of people used in the true personal stories are pseudonyms. The advice and strategies contained herein may not be suitable for every situation and should be considered as general guidance.

"I am for my beloved and my beloved is for me."
– Song of Solomon 6:3

Acknowledgments

I am immensely grateful to all the couples who have welcomed me into their lives. Your stories have been instrumental in my professional growth and learning.

I extend my deepest gratitude to my editor, Steve Donahue, the "book whisperer," whose brilliance shone through in every aspect of refining my message. His unparalleled professionalism, coupled with his encouragement and human touch, have been deeply appreciated.

My sincere appreciation extends to FriesenPress, whose collaboration has been pivotal in bringing this book to life. From the initial stages to the final touches, their team's expertise and dedication have played a critical role in shaping this project. I am deeply grateful for their partnership and the collective efforts of everyone involved.

To my precious friends who share my spiritual journey, your unwavering support and belief in this book have been like pillars of strength. You have shared the ebbs and flows of the process with love and care.

A heartfelt thank-you to Dave Young, who never hesitated to offer his valuable feedback every time I reached out.

And to my beloved husband, Matthew, thank you for the gift of space and time to pursue this endeavor, and for being the enduring love of my life. Our journey continues, and I am thankful for every step we take together.

TABLE OF CONTENTS

INTRODUCTION

"Every human being has both sets of forces within him. One set clings to safety and defensiveness out of fear. The other set of forces impels him forward toward wholeness."
– Abraham Maslow

*O*nce upon a time, I wanted to be an ambassador and help countries "get along" so we could all enjoy a harmonious world full of peace and love. That's why my undergraduate degree is in international relations. When I realized politics weren't for me, I decided to narrow my scope and become a counselor, eventually specializing in working with couples. I thought, perhaps, world peace could be reached through more loving relationships—one couple at a time.

I have been running a thriving private practice as a couples' counselor for over eight years. During this time, I've had the privilege to meet with hundreds of couples, each with their own narratives, hopes, and conflicts. It might surprise you to learn that despite the myriad personalities and circumstances I encounter—at this point in my career—I am seldom taken aback by the stories that unfold within my counseling room walls.

More often than not, couples grapple with such strikingly similar issues and dilemmas, there are moments I wish I could introduce them to each other. A realization they're not alone in their struggles could offer some relief. There is a certain comfort in understanding our problems are normal—even common—and that there's nothing to be ashamed of.

I see a universal pattern—one partner feels unfulfilled and deeply lonely while the other feels inadequate and disappointing, like a failure. One wants to feel more loved and be happier, while the other wants their partner to be happy in the relationship. This dynamic, though unique to each couple in its details, often stems from a fundamental struggle: how to accept and respect each other's differences while simultaneously getting your own needs met. Couples try to "get on the same page," but this endeavor can be tricky, as no one wants to lose themselves in their quest for alignment.

The gnawing emotional hunger to feel closer—seen and heard—isn't easily satisfied. It can seem like a no-win situation. If the lonelier partner chooses to bear their emotional pain in silence, their suffering continues unabated. Voicing their needs and desires, on the other hand, often ignites conflict and further widens the gulf. It's a conundrum. This common struggle can feel like navigating a desert with no clear path to water.

The biggest challenge in my work has been addressing the seemingly infinite list of "dualities" couples are confronted with in their relationships. By duality, I mean the simultaneous existence of two contrasting or opposing characteristics or tendencies in a relationship, like two sides of a coin. Dualities are usually experienced as dilemmas. For example, one partner is more talkative and the other more reserved, or one is tidier and the other messier, creating tension in the relationship.

I refer to these as "duality dilemmas" because the contrasting, and sometimes conflicting, perspectives, emotions, or goals imply that meeting one partner's need seems to be at the expense of the others.

It seems as though one partner is destined to win and the other to lose. Couples explain various "dualities" they wrestle with and ask me to help navigate them. "So, what should we do?" they ask, both looking at me intently with big, blinking eyes, patiently waiting for a clear answer.

Whether the dualities pertain to differences in their emotional and sexual needs, the ways they handle money, or their beliefs about raising children, related dilemmas present themselves over and over, with couple after couple. And dualities are tricky, because at times, they are positive and complementary, fostering balance and richness in the relationship, and other times are negative and conflictual, creating disconnection and repetitive arguments that go nowhere.

Day after day, these typical couple struggles weighed heavily on my heart and mind. While I was successful in my work, I yearned to be able to share something more. I had an insatiable quest to extend my reach further, to delve more deeply into the mysterious complexity of love and connection, and to invite an even more meaningful level of clarity, healing, and joy into the lives of my clients. Surely, there had to be something *more* I could offer them.

Then, one day, I found myself at the local butterfly conservatory with my niece and nephew during March break. It began like any other day, and I was enjoying seeing the world, including butterflies, anew through the eyes of little people. Yet, as the time passed, the day unveiled a captivating fact that set my heart racing and reinvigorated my passion for working with couples.

I became enthralled by what seemed to be impossible: how nature had crafted butterflies—creatures with disproportionately broad wings relative to their small bodies—to master the art of flight. The butterfly's expansive wings meet in the middle at varied points, bend, and move in synchrony above its body, generating a vortex of air that lifts it skyward each time the wings "clap" together.

As I watched and listened, a profound revelation struck me: What if we applied the principle of interdependence to our relationships in a similar way? Could two partners—much like the two sets of wings on a butterfly—unite, meet in the middle, and work together to become stronger and more balanced as a couple?

It dawned on me: The butterfly is a perfect metaphor for a couple. Like a butterfly's interdependent wings, two partners in a relationship, while distinct, are intrinsically connected. They inevitably influence each other for better or for worse since they function as one entity, a single "organism," a couple!

The Greek word for butterfly is psyche which also means soul or spirit, highlighting a dual representation of both the insect and the innermost essence of human beings. The metaphor of the butterfly invites couples to consider their partnership as a transformative, soulful journey where the ultimate connection is not just emotional or physical but spiritual.

As I watched the butterflies in flight, another layer of understanding emerged: Just as a butterfly struggles to fly effectively with a damaged wing, a couple finds it hard to function harmoniously when one partner is in a state of strife. We need one another even more in key moments of stress, crisis, loss, grief, and illness.

Surrounded by colorful, fluttering wings and the chatter of my niece and nephew, I recognized that the issues couples contend with—money, sex, parenting, extended family, workload, and addictions—all orbit around the core theme of "interdependence." This insight profoundly altered my perspective as a couples' counselor, fostering a new vision for my work.

Human beings are subject to natural laws just like the rest of nature, yet we prefer to act as though we can skirt these laws. We're aware of the importance of having a balanced diet, work-life balance, and balancing the budget, but too often, we overlook the critical need to build balance in our relationships.

On one hand, we're drawn toward romantic relationships, driven by a natural instinct for connection and procreation. On the other, we hold back, as we're afraid of sacrificing too much and losing our identities. Where do we draw the line? What's reasonable to expect in terms of sharing and having one's own space? We worry about being too dependent, too independent, and codependent. No one teaches us how to balance individuality with relationship or autonomy with interdependence.

How can you both win?

That's the question I strive to answer in this book. You will learn how to build an interdependent partnership fueled by the strength of four wings: two of yours and two of your partner's. Imagine transcending the limitations of individuality—while still maintaining your unique identity—becoming the wind beneath each other's wings, and feeling confident in your ability to build balance, both *between* you and *within* yourself.

Part One, called "The Caterpillar," explains how we get stuck as couples, including the influence of nature, attraction and its flip side: repulsion, the constraints of human perception, and the ways our minds lead us astray.

Part Two, called "The Butterfly," explores eight core principles of interdependent love, each one complemented by three specific practices, amounting to a comprehensive set of twenty-four tools. Each chapter highlights the duality dilemma that blocks the attainment of the principle and concludes with a simple exercise to get you started.

The Butterfly Blueprint offers more than just guidance; it's an invitation to embark on a journey of shared evolution with your partner. Continue reading so you can understand how to transform your relationship from the limitations of a caterpillar, through the chaos of the chrysalis, into the expansiveness and freedom of a butterfly!

PART ONE: THE CATERPILLAR

"The caterpillar does all the work,
but the butterfly gets all the publicity."
– George Carlin

1

Nature Made Relationships This Way

"The heart has its reasons, of which reason knows nothing."
– Blaise Pascal

*I*t's the greatest con job in the history of human existence. Most of us have been taken in at least once. Others have fallen for nature's sleight of hand multiple times. Time and again, we are willing participants in an obvious swindle because it simply feels too good to turn down. I'm referring, of course, to falling in love.

Bait and switch is probably the best phrase to describe what happens when nature tricks us into thinking we've found true love. From that nail-biting anticipation waiting for the next text to the frantic fussing for that first date, nature is in the *driver's* seat when couples initially get together. You've probably heard the saying "love is blind." But a small tweak might be more accurate: *Lust* is blind. Attraction is the bait and the switch comes later.

We don't just *fall* into love. It's more like we're pushed into it by a sweet, neurochemical mix, including oxytocin, dopamine, and serotonin. These are the hormones behind that intoxicating cocktail of trust, pleasure, happiness, and attachment we feel when we first meet. They are what sync our emotions and behavior so we feel like we've met our soulmate. Compatibility seems to flow effortlessly during the honeymoon phase, as we marvel at shared interests, laugh at similar jokes, and enjoy the same pizza toppings.

The beginning of a relationship is a lot like savoring a delicious piece of chocolate: It's sweet, satisfying, and gives you that delightful, natural high. If you really understood what nature was up to with all this hormonal hoodwinking, you might just burst out laughing and tell your partner, "I love you like chocolate!" But, let's be honest, "chocolate love" is not really about loving your partner at all. It's more about the feel-good vibes generated by neurochemicals. You love to *feel* good.

You could go even further and say, "I love you like fish!" Your partner would probably give you a puzzled look, but think about it: When you "love" fish, it's not like you really care about the fish, right? You love the tantalizing taste! The poor fish meets its end because, well, you're hungry and that fish-and-chips dinner isn't going to make itself!

When we say, "I love you," if we're honest with ourselves, what we really mean is "I *enjoy* you." But please don't feel bad or guilty. Nature made relationships this way for a very good reason. Wanting to feel good and enjoy your partner isn't a crime; it's natural. Afterall, what's the point in being alive if we don't enjoy one another? Besides, we're all in the same boat, so there's nothing to be ashamed of.

The early "butterflies" that characterize the start of a relationship are warmly recalled by couples when I first meet them in couples' counseling. I love asking them about when and how they first met and what originally drew them to one another. A flurry of smiles, giggles, and coy glances are exchanged as they decide who will share first.

Jocelyne's eyes lit up as she exclaimed, "He'd drive all the way from Hamilton to Toronto just to go for coffee!" Nate quickly added,

"We met at a wedding. We talked so much. We've been together ever since. I knew she was the one right away."

Todd and Jen met online. "I loved that she was a musician. I was too," Todd shared with satisfaction. "I loved listening to his recorded music," Jen quickly added without missing a beat.

Amir and Nia met on a blind date. "He was funny and charismatic. He made me laugh," Nia said as she reminisced. "She was the perfect girl," Amir added without hesitation.

In those initial stages of infatuation, rose-colored glasses tend to obscure differences and discrepancies, keeping them hidden from view. Instead, what's amplified is the common ground, as you both, often unconsciously, collude to connect. It's like you're effortlessly gliding into the overlapping circle area in the middle of a Venn diagram, where you feel incredibly aligned, magically on the same page, and superbly synchronized.

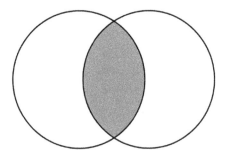

You feel naturally "on the same page"
in the overlapping area when you first meet.

The outlier areas of the two circles—those parts that don't overlap—represent the differences between you and your partner, your opposing characteristics. The *two sides* of the coin are always there, but in your love-struck state, you don't really pay them much attention; you're too busy *feeling* good, you're too busy feeling connected as *the coin*.

Now, imagine the Venn diagram superimposed onto an image of a butterfly. Visualize your relationship as the overlapping area between the two circles or the body of the butterfly. The two outlier areas on the Venn diagram—the left and right sets of wings on the butterfly—represent you and your partner.

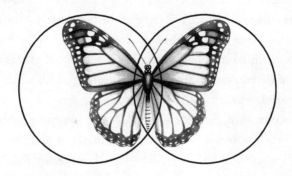

You feel like one organism or a "butterfly" when you first meet.

During the honeymoon phase, your two sets of wings flutter harmoniously as one, reflecting the unity and shared dreams that bring you together. The switch comes after you've taken the bait and the hook is set. After you intertwine your lives in various ways, your bodies adjust and reset. Gradually, you begin to see more than just the overlapping part of the Venn diagram where things seemed so compatible. As the fog lifts, your perception expands to the left and right outlier circle areas that actually oppose one another—the differences between your personalities—and negative feelings begin to arise. The *reality of duality* sets in, minus the hormonal high, leading to disagreements, distance, and disconnection, as though you're no longer reading from the same book, let alone the same page.

After having heard both versions of the "how we met" story, at least one partner in any given couple tends to express a sense of growing deficiency in the relationship. "I feel unimportant, lonely, and empty," I often hear. There is an increasing, insatiable emotional and/or sexual void, like a hunger, inside one or both partners. Expressing this "love lack" evolves into pleading, yelling, and sobbing, and ultimately culminates in the deafening silence of defeat.

As the responsibilities of everyday life take over, often after children have entered the scene, individual preferences, values, and priorities become pronounced. Dr. John Gottman and Dr. Julie Schwartz Gottman joined forces with Doug Abrams and Rachel Carlton Abrams, MD, to present a profound insight in the book, *Eight Dates* (2018). They note that 67% of couples experience a decrease in marital happiness after the birth of their first child, a decline that deepens with each subsequent child. The excessive demands of work and home life make balancing me time, couple time, family time, and social time seem like an impossible endeavor. Something's gotta give, and it's often the couple's connection.

"I just don't know if we're still compatible," Jocelyne admitted. "We've grown apart. We used to do everything together, but after we had kids, we both became more independent. We didn't have a choice, especially since we don't have any family support." Looking down at her hands, she added, "Our lives are so different now. He's always working, and I'm with the kids. I feel like a single parent. I miss the way things used to be, and I'm not sure if we can get that back. It's been lonely for a long time now."

For most couples, trying to talk about the lack of connection devolves into repetitive, circular arguments with no winners. Typically, the partner who feels desperately lonely and unimportant aggressively pursues the other. The other partner—feeling attacked and unappreciated—withdraws and silently hopes all the tension and negativity will simply cease and desist. Eventually, most couples end up feeling like roommates or co-parents and just go through the motions each day. Over time, the relationship continues to deteriorate and eventually comes to a dead end.

Once you've experienced the chemical "flight" of new love, its absence can feel a bit like running out of your favorite chocolate:

painful. The contrast can be dark and bitter, and you may find yourself longing for the excitement and comfort that sweet milk chocolate love had brought into your life. When the spark fades, your drive and motivation to engage with your partner also wane. The honeymoon is officially over. Questions and doubts about compatibility begin to surface.

So, what was all that about anyways? That rollercoaster ride that ended prematurely, leaving you with little but memories, a spinning head, and maybe even an upset stomach? Where did all the love go, and why did it end? And, who's to blame? Were you too much? Or not enough? Are you just unlovable or inadequate? Is your partner even capable of loving you the way you need, or too damaged? Are you really right for each other? Did you ever really love each other in the first place?

When fault lines appear in your relationship, don't worry, it's not your fault. Believe it or not, when the chocolatey sweetness disappears, it's not your partner's fault either. Don't lose hope. Don't despair. It's not the end. In fact, it's just the beginning! It might be hard to grasp it, but when you feel stuck or come to a dead end in your relationship, you are being given an amazing opportunity!

Falling in love is just nature's bait. The truth is that the end of the honeymoon period marks the *real* beginning of your relationship, where you actually learn to *relate* to one another. Most couples believe their love died when the honeymoon ends. They want to try to get things back to the way they used to be when they first met, but they've got it all wrong.

Despite all the swooning novels and gushy songs, the honeymoon phase is actually just a kickstart to the rest of the story, the *true* love story. Mother Nature pushes us together and then pulls us apart over and over again so we will give up on wanting lusty infatuation altogether and come to desire something totally different in its place: *mature love based on wholeness and genuine intimacy.*

In her book *Why We Love* (2022), evolutionary anthropologist Dr. Anna Machin explains that love is a lot like hunger, thirst, and fatigue: It's a physiological motivator that drives us to seek out what we need to survive. Physiological motivators require a "deficiency" or "lack"—like hunger—that is satisfied by some form of fulfillment—like food. The lack and the filling go together like two sides of a coin since a person cannot enjoy food without an appetite, nor would they have an appetite without such a thing as food.

We need to *feel* hungry, thirsty, and—yes—horny so that we will be motivated to eat, drink, and make babies. We need to do all of these things to survive, both individually *and* collectively.

However, as humans, we stand apart in nature; we have the capacity for a higher level of consciousness. This is why mere sexual gratification falls short for us. We want more than the empty calories of sweet, milk chocolate love. We desire deep nourishment and soul fulfillment in our relationships. We want to feel connected inside and out.

Chocolate love is a lot like being a crawling caterpillar, which is okay, but wouldn't you rather be a butterfly? A butterfly possesses four wings—two forewings and two hindwings, or one right set and one left set. The larger forewings primarily provide power while the smaller hindwings offer stability and agility. Though the forewings and hindwings are different in function and size, when they work together, they enable the butterfly to perform a range of vital activities, from feeding to evading predators and mating, in addition to flying.

The different wings work together harmoniously, each contributing its unique function for the butterfly's flight and survival. This interdependence illustrates how distinct elements can collaborate to create a balanced and effective system. This concept helps to clarify how the diverse traits or roles of partners in a relationship can complement each other, enhancing each other's strengths for mutual benefit and fostering harmony. Neither role is superior or inferior; both are necessary for the balance of the overall system, embodying an equality of opposites.

The opposing wings on a butterfly are naturally balanced
and interdependent.

In nature, balance and interdependence manifest automatically in the rhythmic sway of the seasons, each distinct in character yet seamlessly transitioning to the next. This balance is also mirrored in the human body, where various organs each perform their unique functions yet work collectively to sustain the life of the whole. Similarly, in the human brain, there is a dynamic flow between the left hemisphere (logical, linguistic, linear, and literal) and the right hemisphere (contextual, nonverbal, body-oriented, and emotional), each side contributing its unique functions yet simultaneously working together in harmony.

Human beings are the only part of nature required to build balance through effective interdependence consciously and intentionally. Individual and relational balance and wholeness transcend the whimsical satiation of our basic survival instincts and urges.

In the 1940s, psychologist Abraham Maslow created a model of human motivation based on a pyramid. The lower-level needs, like food, sex, and shelter, must be met before higher ones, like self-esteem and belonging, can be pursued.

We take the path of least resistance to ascend on each level, calculating how to get the most fulfillment or pleasure for the least effort. Even when we exert ourselves, it's always for an even greater benefit. For example, we're only willing to study for an exam all night because we desire the pleasurable payoffs of passing the course and attaining a successful career.

Desire constantly grows and changes as it's fulfilled. Satiation on one level leads to a new "lack" on the next level, like climbing a ladder or running on the "hedonic treadmill" of life. We get caught up in an endless loop of striving and attaining, craving and filling, all the way to the top, repeatedly circling back to the default setting of emptiness so we will feel motivated to keep moving forward toward the elusive goal of self-actualization.

Maslow's hierarchy of needs

Human beings are the only part of nature that can get into the *driver's* seat ourselves, and bridge the gaps between what we want and what we have, *intentionally.* We can navigate the two sides *and* the coin—all three points of reference—when we work deliberately and purposefully together. We are capable of experiencing our own uniqueness *and* the closeness we desire in relationship, without diminishing either. We can overcome the bittersweet programming of chocolate love, move beyond gratification for the self alone, and attain true human connection, *consciously*.

Human beings are still evolving. We are in the process of attaining a higher form of *human*—not just mammalian—connection. It's all part of a grand plan to ensure humanity not only survives but *thrives* as one big, interdependent family.

Think of Mother Nature as a loving parent who wants to equip us with everything we need to mature into truly loving adults so we can flourish with all those we hold dear—particularly our life partners. This is why she gave us romantic relationships, which are like mini laboratories in which we can transform from being couples in love to consciously loving couples.

No one said the journey would be easy, though. In every relationship, there comes a time when what was once comfortable becomes conflictual and confusing. This stage mirrors the transformation of a caterpillar into a butterfly, a process that seems chaotic but ends with an awe-inspiring metamorphosis. Your relational struggle is an opportunity for something more meaningful and mutually fulfilling to emerge too: true human connection.

As Susan Cain explains in her book, *Bittersweet*, loss, transience, and the undeniable reality of impermanence shape the contours of our existence, casting light on what truly matters. Mortality, coupled with the inevitable experiences of pain, suffering, adversity, and failure, starkly remind us of life's fragility. These challenges, alongside the acute pangs of longing, the relentless march of time, and the sorrow of separation, serve not merely as harbingers of despair but as profound teachers. Through them, we are compelled to confront the essence of our values, uncover meaning amidst the ephemeral, and deepen our connections. It is precisely this contrast—the ever-present shadow of death—that imbues life with its preciousness. The knowledge that nothing is guaranteed urges us to live more fully, cherish our relationships more deeply, and appreciate the fleeting moments of joy and beauty. In this way, the very forces that might seem to diminish life instead magnify its value, making each moment and connection all the more precious (2022).

In his later years, Maslow added a stage to his hierarchy of needs called self-transcendence. Positioned above self-actualization, it represents the highest level of human development, in which individuals shift from self-centeredness to a broader perspective, where one's actions contribute to the greater good and realization of a purpose beyond the self.

You have a chance—as a couple—to transcend individual limitations and form a new, expansive whole, together. The butterfly incorporates both sets of wings into a greater whole, just like a couple includes two sets of unique attributes and characteristics. The secret to creating a successful relationship lies in how partners approach one another and the space between them.

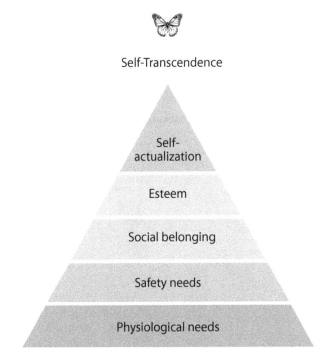

Maslow's hierarchy including self-transcendence

There's magic in the chaos of the chrysalis for both a caterpillar and a couple. The formless soup inside the chrysalis starts to reorganize, "imaginal cells" awaken, new structures emerge, and gradually, a butterfly takes shape. Similarly, through your trials and tribulations as a couple, you can learn new ways to communicate, empathize, and harmonize with one another. With guidance from the Butterfly Blueprint, you can build a stronger, more balanced bond from the ruins of your old relationship. So, relax! Slow down! Take a breath.

Stop reacting. Stop criticizing, defending, and shutting down. Stop beating yourself up and being so hard on your partner. Stop worrying about who is to blame. Mother Nature is to blame! Afterall, she's the one who made relationships this way. Your relationship is normal. What you're going through is the same thing *every* couple goes through to varying degrees, sooner or later, and it's all for a very good reason—so you can share the most abundance possible!

So, embrace your "chrysalis," face your challenges together, and prepare to take flight! Together, you will rise—not by your own strength alone but by the uplifting power of your *shared* efforts. There will no longer be *just* a "you" and a "me"—a vibrant "we" will join the spree—to make three! Together, you will become an embodiment of unity, a symphony, an evolution in harmony!

2

Opposites Attract *and* Repel

"Without contraries is no progression. Attraction and repulsion, reason and energy, love and hate, are necessary to human existence."

William Blake

anjay, with his quiet demeanor, preferred spending evenings curled up with a book. He loved routine, finding solace in the predictable ebb and flow of his life. On the other side of the spectrum was Alejandra, a vivacious woman with a penchant for spontaneous adventures. Her idea of a well-spent day was an unplanned road trip or a surprise salsa dance class.

They had met at a pottery class. Sanjay was intrigued by Alejandra's fiery spirit, and she was drawn to the calming presence he radiated. While Sanjay loved discussing history, Alejandra entertained him with tales of her backpacking adventures across South America. Initially, they were each invigorated by these contrasts.

Their first few months were magnetic, a whirlwind romance of museum dates followed by impromptu backyard bonfires. Sanjay introduced Alejandra to the peace of silent moments, watching sunsets and stargazing. In return, she pulled him into a world where life's unpredictability was its biggest charm.

But with time, their differences began casting shadows. Sanjay sometimes yearned for a quiet weekend, just the two of them, without Alejandra's friends dropping by unannounced. Alejandra, on the other hand, felt slighted when Sanjay declined her last-minute invitations, preferring home and a hot bath.

One evening, after a particularly heated argument about spending yet another weekend apart, they sat down to talk. It was then that they realized the differences that had initially drawn them together were the same ones now fueling their conflicts. Let's take a look at three scientific examples to understand why opposites both attract and repel over the course of time.

* * *

In magnetism, opposing forces demonstrate a dynamic interplay of attraction and repulsion. If you take two magnets and bring their opposite poles—one north and one south—close to each other, they will stick together in a stable, complementary union. This attraction shows how different elements can align perfectly and create a harmonious balance. However, if you try to put two like poles together—two north ends or two south ends—they repel each other. Here, instead of equilibrium, there is imbalance and conflict, leading to a separation.

In a battery, the plus and minus symbols represent the positive and negative terminals, essential for the flow of electric current. When connected in a circuit, the negative electrons are attracted to the positive terminal, creating a stream of energy. Connecting two batteries with the same terminals facing each other, such as positive to positive or negative to negative, blocks the flow. This is because like charges repel each other, leading to a state of imbalance and dysfunction.

Finally, in biological cells, the balance of opposites is vital, as seen in the distribution of positive and negative ions across cell membranes. This ionic balance is essential for critical functions like nerve impulses and muscle contractions, with the outside of cells typically more positive and the inside more negative. This creates potential energy necessary for life processes. However, an imbalance can disrupt cellular functions, resulting in disequilibrium.

The fascinating part about these interactions in magnetism, electricity, and cellular biology is their *dynamic nature*. For example, in cellular biology, the balance of charged ions across cell membranes fluctuates with the cell's environment and its metabolic needs. What begins as an attractive relationship shifts to repulsion as conditions change. This phenomenon mirrors many aspects of our world, from the physics of celestial bodies to the complexities of human relationships.

As explored in Chapter One, the nature of human motivation is also dynamic, continuously growing and evolving over time. The perpetual evolution of desire means that relationships are in a constant state of flux, with both partners continually adapting to shifts in each other's priorities. These changes can draw them closer together or lead to feelings of discord and distance.

The shared, overlapping space in a Venn diagram is therefore not static but dynamically fluctuates, expanding and contracting over time and in different contexts, just like the distinct outlier areas. This ebb and flow reflect the natural progression of a relationship, where the balance of commonalities and differences continuously shifts, mirroring the ever-changing nature of human connections.

This dynamic interplay between attraction and repulsion is what keeps a connection alive and vibrant. However, it can be challenging for couples to navigate their relationships over time, as this requires constant awareness, evaluation, and adjustment. Partners must learn to manage convergence and divergence in their relationship over the course of time. They must negotiate the delicate balance between maintaining their individual identities and fostering a shared life.

"Complementarity Theory," pioneered by psychologist Robert Winch in the 1950s, explains how and why opposites attract in romantic partnerships. According to his work, many people are drawn to partners who possess traits or attributes they lack or admire. For instance, a person who thrives on routine might be attracted to someone who introduces spontaneity, fostering a dynamic where both partners are enriched by the other's contrasting approach. These complementary interactions enhance relational stability and personal development, allowing both individuals to explore and embrace parts of themselves they might have otherwise overlooked or undervalued.

However, while such contrasts can be a source of intrigue and growth, they can also sow the seeds of discord over time. The extroverted tendencies of a partner that once appeared as a refreshing alternative to an introvert's reserved nature, might eventually be perceived as selfish or inconsiderate. These traits can shift from being complementary to becoming sources of misunderstanding, confusion, conflict, and aversion when they diverge too sharply from one's core values or comfort zones.

During the honeymoon phase, it seems as though we are compatible with our partners and there's no such thing as opposing forces or differences—at least nothing that gets in the way of the overall connection. After the switch (in nature's bait and switch tactic), we feel cheated, as though something was taken away, when what's really happening is the lustful fog is clearing to reveal the structure of reality: *duality*.

The problem is that when couples first encounter the "switch," they usually do one of two things: either ignore the differences and pretend everything is fine, or try to actively negate and undermine their partner's opposing perspective. It's natural to feel somewhat threatened by what is different, and it's normal to defend the validity and superiority of one's own position or interests. The problem is that by doing so, we set ourselves up against Mother Nature herself, by trying to sidestep or conquer the reality of duality.

Humanity likes to think we're separate from nature and can live outside of it, but we're subject to natural laws just like all other life forms. We can either go along with the rules that are based on balance and interdependence or go against them. We can learn the rules of the game the easy way or the hard way. We can pay now—upfront, freely, and proactively—or pay later, painfully, under duress, and with interest!

When you try to get your own way, regardless of the impact on your partner, you shoot yourself in the foot—or in the wing. Afterall, how can a butterfly fly with only one set of wings or a damaged set of wings? How can one set of wings *win* over the other? Similarly, in a couple, if one partner loses, both lose because the partner who gets their way will have to confront the frustration, disappointment, and growing resentment of the other partner sooner or later. Romantic relationships must have two winners or no one wins. *Love cannot live without two; love is the glue that bonds opposites.*

Most people come to couples' counseling asking for help with communication, but this is often just the tip of a much deeper problem. People get caught up in repetitive, cyclical arguments about money, parenting, sex, and other issues, which distract from the real issue at hand, the root cause. Even understanding the "process" of arguments (attack, defend, shutdown) and recognizing triggers related to past traumas doesn't resolve the dilemmas couples face. This is like treating the symptoms, rather than the disease.

People want answers, tools, guidance, and solutions. They want to know *what* to do and why they should do it. Above all, they want to be told *how* to move forward in a positive way. The fundamental factor is that in order to progress successfully as couples, we must accept the *reality of duality* and learn how to rise above gaps together, consciously aiming for true human connection—genuine intimacy based on balance, interdependence, and mutual wholeness.

The key to resolving conflicts in relationships isn't to eliminate disagreements or distance by negating your partner or yourself—a common but ineffective approach. This occurs when one partner dismisses, discounts, or disregards the other's feelings and needs, or when one person does this to themselves because they feel guilty when they consider their own feelings and needs. In a healthy relationship, both partners are equals, neither superior or inferior.

Much like yin and yang, the masculine and feminine energies within relationships don't signify superiority or inferiority but, rather, complementary, interdependent forces. One partner's assertiveness or boldness is balanced by the other's softer nurturing nature. Similarly, the logical perspective of one harmonizes with the emotional depth of the other.

The potential for conflict arises when partners are confronted with their differences. The point where their differences converge between them doesn't have to result in a clash. Rather, the distance between partners can be a source of vitality and a hidden treasure, depending on how each partner navigates and manages the differences.

When both parties in a relationship stubbornly try to bend the other to their own will, it often leads to escalating conflict. Over time, this can drive a wedge between them, causing them to grow apart. In the end, this persistent strife is likely to result in separation. On the other hand, if they acknowledge their inevitable impact on one another, for better or for worse, and recognize their mutual dependence—their interdependence—they open up the possibility of another, *revolutionary* way forward—together, better than ever. Their approach to the relationship determines the outcome, whether conflict escalates or peace blossoms.

The space between partners defines each one's individuality, creating the foundation for a relationship between the two. Recognizing your unique traits doesn't imply incompatibility; rather, it's this very distinction that makes a relationship feasible. Without the gap between you, there's no room for interaction and connection. It's the contrast between you that sets the stage for a dynamic relationship to flourish in the in-between space.

Respecting, acknowledging, and valuing your partner's equal and opposite characteristics are key in attaining a positive future together. You get to know yourself and your partner, your set of wings and theirs, as well as the common ground between you. Engaging in such an interdependent connection leads you to a mutually beneficial relationship in which you both win!

We cannot deny that opposites both attract and repel. However, by choosing to come together consciously, we accept and embrace the inherent duality of existence. In doing so, we align with nature's laws and transform our approach from resistance to a harmonious synergy of cooperation and mutual inspiration. Relationships are more than just the sum of individuals; they represent a collective "we," a powerful union that transcends individuality.

3

We Perceive Branches, Not Roots

"What we see depends mainly on what we look for."
– John Lubbock

*T*here is a crossroads couples arrive at once the honeymoon phase has run its course. Most want to return to the way they were when they first met. They stay stuck in the memory of their lost "Garden of Eden," fantasizing about reclaiming that elusive honeymoon vibe. One could imagine this path as going in reverse, heading backwards in time and space. Other couples try to resolve their relationship dilemmas by criticizing and blaming one another to the point that the relationship becomes an endless grudge match, a war of attrition, where each person tries to bend and change the other. Many partners cope with disconnection by engaging in distractions, immersing themselves in various "third things" such as excessive work, gambling, focusing on children, home renovations, hobbies, social media, gaming, porn, overeating, drugs, alcohol, and even affairs. The COVID-19 pandemic posed a particular challenge for the latter as their usual diversions vanished, leaving them face-to-face with the issues they had been adeptly avoiding.

Regardless of the ways couples cope, when the honeymoon phase comes to an end, challenges arise swiftly, largely due to the most mysterious and pervasive duality of all: How what is *internal*, covert, and concealed affects what is *external*, overt, and revealed. You might have heard about the "tip of the iceberg" metaphor. We often only perceive a fraction of reality—the tip—in any given situation. Most of what we need to be aware of remains unseen beneath the waterline, and that hidden part of the story can cause a lot of trouble. Just think of the Titanic.

We only perceive the tip of the iceberg in life and relationships.

I prefer to describe the mysterious duality of what is *internal and external* using the image of a tree, replete with its branches and roots. Just like the iceberg, the branches and roots depict the duality that exists between something hidden and something visible. The branches represent the relatively conscious world, what we know and can perceive using our five senses. The roots delve deep into the unconscious realm—hidden—but equally important to the nourishment and functioning of the tree as a whole. This is where feelings, thoughts, desires, memories, values, beliefs, and bodily sensations reside—any part of experience that we do not perceive using the five senses. Humans live in these two interdependent worlds—the internal and the external—simultaneously.

Part One: The Caterpillar

We live in two worlds at the same time: the external, revealed world of branches and the internal, concealed world of roots.

I like the image of a tree better than the cold, lurking danger of the iceberg because roots and branches imply mutual reliance, interdependent life, and the potential for growth and development. The branches of the tree depend on the roots to provide water and nutrients. The roots rely on the branches and leaves to conduct photosynthesis, which generates the essential sugars and energy necessary for growth and further nutrient absorption.

Just as a coin has two sides, a butterfly flourishes with two symmetrical sets of wings, and a tree thrives through the interdependence of its roots and branches, life hinges on the interactions between the internal and external aspects of our shared experience. Without the contrast of duality, there is no life in life. Together, the revealed and concealed worlds form the very essence of love's mystery.

The internal-external duality confronts every couple sooner or later. The covert world holds myriad factors that influence how you interact with your partner and how your partner interacts with you. Trauma echoes emotionally from the past into the present. Perhaps there's a previous relationship that inflicted a deep wound, leading one of you to be cautious about fully opening up to the other. Maybe there are insecurities from childhood that trigger defensive reactions and emotional walls. There could even be dreams or aspirations that have yet to be shared, leading to isolation or misunderstandings.

When we think the world of branches is all there is, we become stuck. When we don't acknowledge or are out of touch with the potentially subversive, hidden realm of roots, things can feel out of control, like the tail's wagging the dog.

Look at the contrast between what Pat and Bill say in the external world of branches (the quotes) versus what they think and feel in the internal world of roots (underneath):

Pat: Branches: "Can we talk?"

      Roots: I'm so lonely.

Bill: Branches: "What?"

      Roots: Uh-oh, what did I do wrong now?

Pat: Branches: "Why are you working overtime again this weekend?"

      Roots: I'm afraid you don't care about me or want to spend time with me.
I just want to be happy.

Bill: Branches: "My boss asked me. There's no one else who can do it. I was home last weekend!"

      Roots: It doesn't matter what I do, you'll never be happy. I'll never be good enough. What's the point in trying? It doesn't make any difference.

Pat: Branches: "You always make excuses and have a reason! You seem to want to spend your life at work!"

      Roots: Why don't you ever talk to me about these decisions? Include me in your life? I feel so unimportant to you…and empty.

Bill: Branches: "It's not an excuse! Why are you always complaining? You should take up a hobby!"

Roots: Here we go, you're getting upset now. I don't want to argue. I feel that pressure in my chest coming on. Anything I say will just make things worse. This is exactly why I stay at work more lately.

Pat: Branches: "I'm complaining because you're not listening!! You never listen to me! You can't communicate!!"

Roots: I feel so desperate for you to understand how alone I feel.

Bill: Branches: "You're right! I'm the problem! Maybe you should find someone who knows how to communicate!"

Roots: I just want you to be happy. I don't know what to do. I need to get out of here.

Pat: Branches: "There you go again! Leave like you always do! You're so heartless!"

Roots: I'm so angry and hurt that you never put me first. Why do you seem to be so much happier around other people?

Bill: Branches: "Well, I'd rather be anywhere else than here with all this negativity...."

Roots: I'm going to do something I'm good at, spend time with someone who appreciates me, or have some fun so I don't have to feel like such a disappointment and failure.

Many forms of individual and couple's therapy attempt to understand and untangle what lies beneath, in the roots. Carl Jung, the Swiss psychiatrist, introduced the notion of the "shadow," which represents the concealed parts of ourselves we often shy away from acknowledging. These are aspects of the self that we suppress due to their misalignment with our conscious values, social norms, or self-perception. Despite being hidden, these shadow elements profoundly influence our behavior and relationships.

Jung's concept of projection is a perfect example. He believed the characteristics we don't recognize or accept within ourselves are often those that trigger strong reactions in us toward others. When conflicts arise and you find yourself in cycles of blame, criticism, defensiveness, or stonewalling with your significant other, more than likely you are grappling with hidden aspects of your *own* psyche; you're shadow boxing.

For example, if you find yourself irritated by your partner's need to vie for attention, it might hint at a suppressed desire within *you* to be noticed—a part of you that's buried deep, rejected, perhaps due to guilt or shame. If you're exasperated by your partner's lack of organization or their easygoing nature, it might not just be about *their* behavior. It likely reflects your own internal battle: a part of you that wishes to break free, relax, and be spontaneous, but is constrained by your surface-level need to be in control. In these instances, your partner acts as a mirror, reflecting shadows from your roots back at you.

Annoyance with your partner can reveal hidden facets of your own personality that are longing to be discovered, known, and felt, as well as expressed, but are overpowered by more dominant parts. It's easier to place the blame on your partner, to see the antagonist or the "enemy" outside yourself, while failing to acknowledge the corresponding nemesis within. Turning inward means facing deep, unprocessed pain from the past, and who wants to do that?

Ironically, defense mechanisms can result in a self-fulfilling prophecy, where individuals inadvertently create the exact scenarios they dread. For example, an underlying fear of abandonment might manifest in behaviors like being critical or defensive, which, in turn, may cause your partner to run for the nearest exit, thus leaving you feeling—yes—abandoned. Similarly, harboring a deep-seated fear of rejection could lead you to emotionally withdraw or shut down, inadvertently causing your partner to feel unimportant and shut out. This, in turn, might prompt them to respond with criticism or confrontation, bringing about the very rejection you initially feared. In attempting to protect yourself, your defense mechanisms can unintentionally backfire, leading you to re-experience the very pain you sought to avoid, effectively trapping you in a self-created prison.

Due to the concealed world of roots, our perceptions of our partners are rarely accurate. We filter the world, including our partners, through our own unconscious root system: experiences, beliefs, biases, and emotions. These elements act as lenses, shaping and coloring perception, much like a pair of tinted glasses or a magnifying glass alter the way we see our surroundings; certain aspects of reality are magnified while others are distorted and obscured into the background, like how we don't see the stars during the day—but they are still there. What is emphasized or minimized depends on one's own history. Perception is therefore highly subjective—not objective—for all of us.

Differences in perception often give rise to misunderstandings, miscommunication, and conflicts. Assuming your partner shares your inner world and thoughts can lead to the unrealistic expectation that they should intuitively understand your needs and feelings; that they can read your mind, or your roots. This belief sets the stage for frustration and disconnection.

Chloe, who identified as a "people-pleaser," didn't like to ask for what she wanted, as she didn't want to be a burden to her partner, Kim. She also didn't like saying "no," as she didn't want Kim to feel hurt or rejected. Chloe thought Kim would understand this "obvious" approach to relationships; however, Kim actually found this exceedingly aggravating. Kim wanted to know how to get things right with Chloe and hated having to play guessing games to figure out what she wanted. Kim wanted Chloe to ask directly for what she wanted and to be clear and truthful when she said "yes" or "no" so that Kim would then be able to trust that when Chloe said "yes," she actually meant it!

People also often believe that if their partner would just handle situations and other relationships the same way they do themselves, everything would work out for the better. This is often the case with those partners who self-identify as "fixers." Fix-it mode discounts your partner's unique personality, values, and roots, and leads to misunderstandings and tension over time. For example, when one partner easily and simply solves problems at work by putting their foot down, this doesn't mean the same cut-and-dried approach will work for the other partner at *their* job. This issue came up with Mark and Joanne.

"You just have to say 'no' and set some boundaries!" Joanne explained to Mark, who was working more and more overtime. She continued, "It's not your problem if deadlines aren't met. That's why the managers get paid the big bucks!!" Mark seemed to be in his own world, looking off to the side, when he quietly added, "It's just not that easy. If I want to be promoted, I have to prove myself," hinting at the deeper longings and fears that were rooted in his decision to work overtime.

Many people put up a tough front in the world of branches but suffer in silence on the inside, in their roots. This juxtaposition of outward resilience and inner fragility underscores the intricate and multi-layered nature of human experience.

Take Priya's case, for instance. She often wrestles with feelings of insecurity, yet she keeps these emotions hidden from others. During a counseling session, when her tears begin to flow, her husband,

Aarav, is taken aback. In disbelief, he exclaims, "Who is this? I never see this side of you. It feels like you're just acting this way because we're in counseling. You always seem so strong and capable, and mostly, you're just angry with me. Seeing you cry like this…It's hard to believe!"

You might find yourself judging your partner's reactions as "too sensitive" or "dramatic," unwittingly invalidating their deeper, concealed thoughts and emotions. Such judgments can inadvertently undermine your partner's authentic emotions, which stem from aspects of their personality that may not be readily visible or expressed. This was the case with Tom and Mike.

After Tom received negative feedback from his boss and became visibly upset, Mike wondered out loud, "I don't get why you're so worried about it. You're just overthinking and making excuses not to go to work. Get over it and move on!" Tom, doing his best to articulate his feelings, responded, "It's not about the feedback itself. It's about how it was delivered and the context around it." Mike, not considering Tom's roots, shot back, "You're playing the victim again, just like you always do."

Mike failed to acknowledge that hidden facets of Tom's past—specifically his relationship with his authoritative father—played a significant role in Tom's reaction to his boss. The boss's domineering and critical communication style echoed that of Tom's father, triggering ingrained feelings of inadequacy and defensiveness in Tom. He had very good reasons for his strong emotions when the past was put into the equation.

During arguments, couples often find themselves embroiled in debates about details: the who, what, when, where, why, and how of what happened. Much of this contentious dialogue is focused on the external world of actions or branches. These debates are fueled by a battle of perceptions and often sound like splitting hairs during couples' counseling sessions.

"It was in the afternoon," Sandra emphasized.

"No, it was in the morning, at 11:30," Brad retorted.

"You said you'd come home after work!" Carly shouted.

"I *did* come home after work! I just stopped to grab a few groceries on the way!" Ahmed refuted.

Each partner ardently defends their version of reality, firmly believing they are right. Arguments fall into the "content trap," a debate about minutiae, much like arguing about which way the deck chairs were arranged on the *Titanic* as it silently slipped beneath the surface into the cold, dark waters.

Beneath the quagmire of disputes couples get caught up in, what gets overlooked is the realm of roots—the concealed forces guiding how each partner shows up on the surface. Even as we vehemently stand our ground over trivial details, the deeper, unseen aspects of our longings and fears are pulling the strings, governing our responses, like the Wizard of Oz behind a curtain.

We hesitate to acknowledge we're largely in the dark about these root-level influences that shape all of us. Instead of embracing a humbler attitude and admitting how much we don't know, we find ourselves entangled in a web of assumptions, theories, appraisals, and speculations. The tendency to analyze and diagnose leans more toward hubris than humility, and consequently impedes our ability to truly connect.

You're likely starting to understand the significant impact of the pervasive internal-external duality on relationships. Yearning to return to the Shangri-La of the honeymoon stage, discounting our partners or ourselves, and engaging in distractions all prove to be insufficient when it comes to getting where we want to be. This is because the world of roots is elusive like shifting sands in the desert and largely beyond our control.

Also, getting to know and understand our roots systems still doesn't *directly* address the main question asked by so many clients: "So, what should we *do*?"

The typical ways we cope with duality also fail to address another obvious question: What on earth was Mother Nature thinking when she concealed the world of roots? Why do it? Is she a sadist? Life could be so much easier and simpler if we could perceive the whole "tree" of interdependent life and live together with our partners in a single world. We would be able to see our similarities—how we're on the same page—clearly. And we'd be able to see the mine fields, the no-go, danger zones that are off limits, without confusion. We'd know *my partner isn't that deep no matter how much I dig, so I might as well stop*, or, *my partner is sensitive, so I should tread lightly here*. Why make life so we have one foot in the branches and the other in the roots? It makes life so unnecessarily complicated and complex!

Navigating reality is like an "escape room" game partners have to solve *together*. By collaborating and combining their strengths, they can transcend the limitations of individuality. It's this collective effort that unlocks the door to a reality rich in fulfillment for both, yielding the prize of a deeper, more profound experience.

And herein lies the secret of human life! Human beings are a unique part of nature with a special purpose. We live in two worlds simultaneously so that we will come to see that *we need one another whether we like it or not. We depend on each other to become whole whether we want to or not.*

Also, we have a capacity for consciousness that animals do not. While some animals have been shown to exhibit signs of awareness of what is external such as recognizing themselves in a mirror, like elephants, dolphins, and some great apes, the depth and complexity of this awareness are more pronounced in humans. We have a much greater capacity for abstract thought, including imagining the future and metacognition—the ability to think about our own thoughts. We have the potential to perceive what is outside of our own bodies.

All the other levels in nature are balanced automatically. A caterpillar does not have to make a conscious effort to transform, through the chaotic process inside the chrysalis, into a beautiful butterfly.

It just happens. Similarly, a forest ecosystem naturally maintains its balance, with each species playing its role in the cycle of life without conscious effort, contributing to the overall harmony and sustainability of its environment.

However, unlike these natural processes, humans must *consciously* work to reconcile their differences. Humans have the capacity to act as connectors or adaptors, integrating and balancing the variations between us. Each partner's characteristics play an essential role, much like every element in nature, meaning there are no "bad guys" in the system. It is through deliberate effort that we harmonize these differences to maintain the health of our relationships.

I view the internal-external duality as a crucial factor impacting human development and evolution. In the overt world—the world of branches—we each exist individually. However, this perceived separation is merely surface-deep. When we delve beneath, into the covert world—the world of roots—we are much more interconnected than we realize or care to admit.

This is why "fix it" mode doesn't work. We try to improve the relationship externally, from the outside in, without realizing that true change comes from within. When we shift our own attitude and approach, it influences the entire relationship system. This internal shift impacts how our partner responds, leading to a change in the relationship dynamic. By adopting "systems" thinking, we can foster more profound and effective changes in our relationships.

Remember, you're never just a passenger in your relationship. As an integral part of the butterfly, your actions and words, or lack thereof, significantly impact your partner, the other set of wings. It's akin to the organs in a body, where each has a crucial role. Imagine if the lungs decided not to provide oxygen, dismissing the heart's needs as "selfish," or if the heart stopped pumping blood, criticizing the lungs' protest for being "dramatic." Just as each organ is vital to the body's health, your roles in the relationship are equally important. Every move you make affects this shared entity, whether you intend it to or not. You're a part of a single, living organism where every part is interconnected and essential.

In fact, it is known that the roots of trees communicate with each other. According to a study conducted by Suzanne Simard at the University of British Columbia, trees in a forest exchange nutrients and information through an underground network of fungi, a phenomenon known as the "Wood Wide Web." Life forms are not as isolated as they appear to be above ground. All life thrives on interconnectedness, and humans are no exception to the universal law of interdependence.

By properly relating to each other with an interdependent attitude in which both partners are viewed as equally valuable, we pave the way to authentic connection. Deep, human intimacy isn't just rooted in mutual attraction or shared experiences, but in a wholeness that includes and incorporates what we perceive *and* what our partner perceives, what comes from the inside out *and* what comes from the outside in.

Just as the roots and branches of a tree are indispensable to its entirety, so too are the perspectives of *both* partners in a relationship. Remember, a couple, by definition, requires two. It takes a "you" and a "me" to make a "we," or *three*—like having a new baby—which transcends duality: *two* parts that, together, make up *one* wondrous whole.

The magic unfolds when, instead of reacting to your partner, trying to change them, or avoiding the differences between you, you rise above a self-absorbed, chocolate-love approach and start to see your partner as the gift they truly are. Seeing your partner as a mirror that reflects your deeper self provides a precious opportunity for personal growth and transformation. Caring for the connection between you demonstrates enlightened self-interest.

Your partner is the key that can unlock the door to a realm of much deeper intimacy inside and out. When couples master an interdependent approach to connection, they set a precedent and pave the way for larger communities and even countries to come together in harmony. As couples, we are not just evolving for ourselves but are helping to shape the future of all humanity!

4

We Tell Ourselves Stories

"The universe is made of stories, not of atoms."
– Muriel Rukeyser

The best stories always have a villain—it's a person or a group of people or a thing that all the protagonist's problems can be attributed to. Perhaps that's why I often see this relieved look on the faces of couples when I explain that nature is the villain in their story. Finally, they can stop blaming themselves and each other!

Indeed, Mother Nature is the orchestrator behind the scenes, crafting relationships with a complex, sometimes confounding, design. She draws us together with a surge of hormones, then shifts the terrain with the bait-and-switch manoeuvre. As outlined in Chapter One, physiological motivators spur our development by introducing a deficiency and its corresponding fulfillment—like the pang of hunger met with food, or the ache of loneliness soothed by companionship. Mother Nature ensures that opposites both attract and repel over time, and she is the one who placed us between two worlds: the tangible world of branches and the hidden world of roots, challenging us with limited and distorted perception.

But like all good villains, Mother Nature isn't all bad. She equipped us with tools for survival and development as a species. She also gave us everything we need to *thrive*, collectively, even if we have yet to fully grasp the workings of the system. We know the goal is to live interdependently together, as couples, communities, and even countries. But the question still remains, *how?*

Part Two of the Butterfly Blueprint is my best effort to put forth a vision of how we can live interdependently as couples. In the meantime, we were given a way to make sense out of what the hell is going on around here: storytelling. When the fairy tale honeymoon story has run its course, we naturally craft new stories to understand our evolving selves, our partners, and our relationships, filling the void with tales that redefine the post-honeymoon world.

For instance, consider the story of Leah and Ryan. Leah frequently told herself, "Ryan is always so distant and uninterested." This story stemmed from Ryan's quiet demeanor during conflicts, which Leah interpreted as disinterest. However, in Ryan's mind, his silence was a way to avoid escalating arguments, a lesson learned from observing his parents' volatile disputes. Ryan's internal narrative was "If I stay quiet, I can keep the peace." Both Leah and Ryan's stories shaped their understanding of their interactions, despite being based on misconceptions.

Stories play a crucial role in constructing one's identity and worldview. Each of us carries a unique set of beliefs, values, and assumptions that shape how we perceive the world and how we define our place in it. Our personal narratives embody these beliefs and values, reflecting who we are, where we come from, and where we're going; they give us a sense of continuity and coherence, providing a stable and consistent map of sorts that guides our interactions in the world.

According to Dr. John Gottman and Nan Silver, the manner in which couples reminisce about and describe their shared history—the story of how they met, their early days of dating, challenges they've faced, and memorable moments they've shared—can serve as an indicator of the strength and health of their relationship.

Gottman and Silver determined that the manner in which couples describe their shared past—specifically the level of positivity, affection, and respect evident in their stories—offers insight into the success or failure of their relationship in the future (1999).

The storytelling function within our brains touches all aspects of our lives, not just our relationships. Conspiracy theories are an extreme manifestation of the storytelling instinct. In a world marked by uncertainty and rapid change, conspiracy theories offer simplistic narratives that promise certainty and control. They propose clear villains, straightforward solutions, and a sense of order. However, they also highlight the potential dangers of our storytelling instinct, showing how it can lead us astray. And let's be honest— some people literally become *conspiracy theorists* in their relationships, going to great lengths to construct a narrative that explains the dysfunction by framing their partner as the culprit!

In fact, we all become a bit like bad-guy detectives, observing our partners carefully, interpreting their words and actions, and constructing stories to explain their behavior. But we don't just make up stories about *them*—we also tell ourselves stories about who we are and how we fit into the relationship. Some of the most common stories I hear over and over again are

- My partner doesn't care.
- There must be something wrong with me.
- I'm a disappointment. I'm a failure.
- My partner is incapable of giving me what I need.
- My partner will never be happy no matter what I do.

The stories we tell ourselves often revolve around justifying our own feelings or actions and making assumptions about our partners' motives. For example, one partner might think, "He didn't do the dishes because he doesn't respect my time," rather than considering alternative explanations. Another might think, "I'm just a chore, an obligation, an item ticked off her checklist," when she tries to meet his needs. My favorite is "She just wants to fight," when the partner raises issues. These kinds of narratives increase resentment and distance, and add to negative cycles.

Dr. Marshall Rosenberg, a psychologist and author of *Nonviolent Communication* (2015), highlights a common misconception in communication. He writes that when we think we are expressing feelings, we're usually giving opinions, interpreting, evaluating, hypothesizing, assessing, and judging our partners—all of which are activities that essentially boil down to telling ourselves stories. The following list of words we use to express ourselves are not feeling words; they are more interpretive and evaluative than feeling-based. We say things like, "I feel…"

- Unheard
- Abandoned
- Abused
- Attacked
- Betrayed
- Bullied
- Manipulated
- Neglected
- Pressured
- Rejected
- Taken for granted
- Threatened
- Unappreciated
- Unwanted

We also often express thoughts disguised as feelings: *I feel like you don't care.* Usually, we're telling our partners about themselves rather than opening up about ourselves. Emotions (and clear statements of need) typically get buried and lost under layers of unbridled, subjective storytelling.

If you don't use emotional labels, you're not expressing feelings. Paul Eckman identified the following fundamental emotions in the 1970s:

- Happiness
- Sadness
- Anger
- Surprise
- Disgust
- Pride
- Shame
- Embarrassment
- Excitement
- Fear

We often avoid expressing and owning our emotions. It's hard to actually feel painful feelings in our own bodies. It can make us feel vulnerable, weak, needy, and childlike; we don't want to be seen as less-than. Also, emotions, in conjunction with mind, give us clues about what we need to do, which subsequently makes us more responsible. It's easier and more comfortable to play the victim card and expect others to change so we can feel better.

Thoughts and feelings are closely intertwined, again, kind of like two sides of a coin. It's easy to see how the stories we tell ourselves can be transmuted into our deepest core fears. The thought "I'm not good enough" could be rephrased as "I'm afraid I'm not good enough." Similarly, "I'm a failure" can be translated as "I'm afraid I'm a failure." Many of us learned to suppress our emotions and are relatively unaware of the emotional energy within us. This emotional energy might manifest somatically, presenting as a stomach ache, a heavy feeling in the chest, or a lump in the throat.

Attachment theory also provides insights into how individuals tell themselves stories in relationships. People with different attachment styles tend to create stories that align with their expectations of relationships. For instance, an anxiously attached individual might interpret a partner's need for space as abandonment, while an avoidantly attached person might view a request for more intimacy as clinginess or intrusion.

Heavily influenced by the concepts of story and identity, narrative therapy encourages clients to examine, externalize, and modify the prevailing narratives they've internalized. This process involves identifying negative or limiting beliefs and "re-authoring" their story in a way that promotes empowerment, resilience, hope, and well-being. While narrative therapy can be beneficial, at the end of the day, it still traffics in storytelling—it's just that the story gets a little better.

The structure and function of the human brain also play pivotal roles in shaping the stories we tell ourselves. Confirmation bias is the tendency to focus on information that supports one's existing beliefs while disregarding anything contradictory. When applied to relationship narratives, this can lead to selective recall or interpreting events in ways that reinforce pre-existing perceptions and expectations. For instance, if you believe that your partner is always late, you might pay more attention to the times when they arrive late and overlook the instances when they are on time. This skewed perception can exacerbate misunderstandings and disconnection in your relationship.

The OATS brain circuitry was introduced by Dr. Dan Siegel in his book, *Mind* (2017). OATS, an acronym for "others and the self," refers to the human brain's default mode of operation, where it's constantly interpreting experience in relation to oneself and others. This nonstop inner dialogue helps us make sense of the world by linking what we perceive and feel to thoughts and memories. Siegel explains that the brain creates "maps" of perception, which form the basis of our beliefs about ourselves, our partners, and our relationships. The problem is that these maps are heavily influenced by past experience and memory. Instead of interpreting new information objectively, the human brain uses these maps or mental scripts to shape our understanding, further distorting perception.

For example, if you've had experiences where your trust was broken, your brain might be wired to be on high alert, interpreting your partner's innocent actions as deceitful, even if they have no malevolent motive. This is because the brain is designed to recognize patterns, detect danger, and protect us from perceived threats. Ingrained memories and stories, therefore, dictate how we react in the present, often without conscious awareness.

As a result, we can easily fall into repetitive patterns, letting old wounds dictate our current reactions and inadvertently casting shadows over fresh opportunities to build trust, understanding, and connection. We interpret experience negatively through the lens of pre-existing stories, which are further shaped and refined by our bleak experiences. We get caught in a self-perpetuating feedback loop that keeps us imprisoned in the past.

This happened to John and Lisa, who, like so many other couples, found themselves ensnared in a complex Catch-22 around emotional and sexual connection. Lisa craved emotional intimacy as a prerequisite for physical closeness, while John felt a passionate sexual connection would naturally lead to deeper emotional bonding.

This interlocking dynamic presented a conundrum that left them both feeling lost and alone. Such a stalemate generated a whirlwind of questions, doubts, uncertainties, and—yes—stories! They each filled in the blanks, trying to make sense out of what was happening. The stories they were telling themselves obscured the real issues at play, further complicating their path toward authentic emotional and sexual intimacy. Let's take a look at their typical related conversation:

Lisa: "John, I feel like you dismiss me as too sensitive or dramatic. It's not just in my head. I'm not neurotic." (Stories: My family always told me I was overreacting. My ex said I was too demanding. I feel like I'm never heard, just like back then. John's just like them, making me feel like I'm too much.)

John: "Lisa, I think we should focus on the positives, not dwell on the negatives. That's how things get solved." (Stories: My family avoided conflict. We never talked about our issues. I feel overwhelmed when Lisa spirals into what's wrong. I'm trying to be positive, but nothing I do is ever good enough for her.)

Lisa: "You always walk away from our conversations. It feels like you see me as a burden." (Stories: My ex would shut down when things got serious. I feel the same with John. It's like he doesn't care enough to stay and understand.)

John: "When I do something wrong, you just get more upset. It feels like you're always trying to change me." (Stories: My parents were never happy with what I did. Now with Lisa, it's like walking on eggshells all over again. I just agree, to keep the peace, but it never works.)

Lisa: "You expect sex without caring about my emotional needs. Can't you see that?" (Stories: My previous partner only showed affection when he wanted something. I feel used with John. He doesn't seem to care about what I need emotionally.)

John: "I don't expect anything. I deal with things on my own. I don't want to burden you or make you more stressed." (Stories: I've always kept my problems to myself. My parents never shared their worries either. Lisa's problems seem so big, and I don't know how to help. I'm disappointing her. No wonder she doesn't want me anymore.)

In this scenario, John and Lisa are each trapped in the stories they tell themselves, which are shaped by past experiences. Lisa's history of feeling dismissed and too emotional leads her to perceive John's actions as uncaring. John, conditioned to avoid conflict and internalize his emotions, feels unable to meet Lisa's needs and overwhelmed by her expectations. He sees himself as disappointing and failing her. These stories create a cycle of misunderstanding, confusion, and chaotic communication.

In a previous chapter of your life, your stories probably served as shields, like armor, protecting you from potential harm or guiding you through tough situations as a child or in past relationships. However, as you enter new phases of your life, these same stories represent obsolete roadblocks, obstructing the path to deeper connection and understanding.

Imagine navigating your relationship with an old map, one that doesn't account for the new "roads" and "landscapes" you and your partner are exploring together. Clinging to outdated stories is like insisting on using that old map, despite its irrelevance to your current journey. These narratives, once comforting and familiar, now stand as barriers to genuine intimacy and growth.

It's important to recognize when a once-helpful story or set of beliefs has outlived its usefulness. Perhaps it's a belief that vulnerability is a weakness or a conviction that seeking help is a sign of failure. These stories, though they might have shielded you in the past, now prevent you from fully engaging with your partner and embracing the richness of your shared experience.

Transforming your relationship means questioning these stories you tell yourself; you need to doubt the capacity of your mind. This involves pausing, reflecting, and asking yourselves: "What is the story I'm telling myself?" "How is the present different from the past?" "How is my partner different from my parents or my ex?" and "How am I different from who I was back then, as a child or in my past relationship?" Trusting the accuracy of the stories you tell yourself can lead you further away from your goal of having a fulfilling relationship.

However, merely letting go of the stories we tell ourselves isn't enough to make significant change in our relationships. In my work with couples, the goal isn't to craft a new or better story. Instead, it's about transcending the act of storytelling altogether. My approach requires that you open your heart and redirect your focus from the individually oriented perspectives of "you" and "me" to a collective, higher pursuit: interdependent connection.

Mother Nature got us all into the messiness of romantic love. *She* is the one who made relationships this way. *She* made opposites attract *and* repel. *She* designed the dual worlds we inhabit—the internal and external worlds of roots and branches. And *she* also gave us the capacity to tell ourselves stories to make some sense out of life. While Mother Nature might seem like the villain or the bad guy, the silver lining is that she also holds the key to unravel our relational puzzles, quandaries, and duality dilemmas.

Albert Einstein said, "Look deep into nature, and then you will understand everything better." Part Two of this book draws inspiration and direction from nature's ultimate masterpiece: the butterfly. The metaphor of a butterfly is used as a blueprint for creating healthy interdependent relationships with the guidance of eight principles and 24 practices. Like a butterfly emerging vibrant and transformed from its chrysalis, you can experience a similar metamorphosis through this approach. By embracing the tools and strategies in the Butterfly Blueprint, you can flourish in your partnership, embarking on an exciting, new, shared journey of growth and love.

PART TWO: THE BUTTERFLY

"Humanity is one integral, interconnected organism,
and our future depends on our realizing this."
– Dr. Michael Laitman

INTRODUCTION

"Interdependence is a fundamental law of nature.
Even tiny insects survive by cooperating with each other.
Our own survival is so dependent on the help of others
that a need for love lies at the very core of our existence."
– The Dalai Lama

Imagine a scene where people are seated around a table laden with delicious food yet are frustrated and starving. Everyone has long spoons that reach the food, but they are too long to bring the nourishment to their own mouths. In one version of this allegory, it is depicted as Hell—a place of abundance that becomes stricken with scarcity due to the inability of the individuals to feed themselves. In another version, the exact same situation is depicted as Heaven (or, hea-VENN). Here, the people use their long spoons to feed each other *across* the table. This simple shift in aim transforms a place of starvation and despair into one of joy and abundance.

In my own work as a couples' counselor, I use the allegory of the long spoons to teach the value of interdependence—the recognition that we thrive best as human beings when we support one another. Caring for the connection between partners—the relationship—benefits *both* individuals since they each rely on it for their own pleasure and enjoyment.

49

Interdependence forms the foundation of the Butterfly Blueprint. This is more than a self-help buzzword. Interdependence has been researched extensively since the publication of the ground breaking book *The Social Psychology of Groups* in 1959. In it, psychologists John Thibaut and Harold Kelley wrote that people's behavior is influenced by what they expect to get from their interactions with others. These expectations subsequently affect how people *depend* on each other and guide their decisions in a group.

Interdependence theory reveals how interactions with others are driven by the anticipation of costs and benefits. This "bottom-line" approach is an ingrained aspect of human nature. We are constantly calculating and evaluating the potential costs and benefits of our actions *for ourselves*, and these expectations frequently guide our decisions and behaviors, just like the chocolate-love approach to relationships we discussed in Chapter One. We consistently ask ourselves two key questions, "What's in it *for me?*" and "Is it worth it?"

Thibaut and Kelley further developed their theory in the 1978 book *Interpersonal Relations: A Theory of Interdependence.* They examined interdependence in one-on-one relationships, introducing factors like cooperation, competition, and power dynamics, and found that as relationships deepen over time, motivation tends to shift from personal gain to a focus on positive joint outcomes. They noted that this shift was a vital evolution in order to sustain close relationships.

The *transformation of motivation* from self to mutual benefit is the key shift couples need to make when the honeymoon phase ends. The moment you hit that crucial crossroads and duality dilemmas arise, the transformation of your motivation is what will set you on the right path toward a bright future. Gaps appear between you, and it's your job to bridge them consciously, together.

Like the shift to feeding *one another* with the long spoons, the well-being of the relationship as a whole needs to become the focus for *both* partners. Just as a butterfly depends on its body to coordinate the left and right sets of wings, strengthening and balancing the connection between two partners is of paramount importance in a healthy couple. If only one partner engages in this approach, the other will "starve." However, one partner can still lead the way and show the other how it's done—how to balance or compromise in a way that respects and integrates both partners' needs. It's the job of the other to follow suit.

Consider a situation where one partner wants to watch a particular movie but knows their partner would enjoy a different movie more. If they were acting solely on self-benefit, they would insist on watching their own preference. But if they shift their motivation, they might decide to watch their partner's top choice. They would still experience some enjoyment *through* the enjoyment of the other because of the love they share.

On the other hand, if you are a people-pleaser and tend to put yourself last—out of guilt and fear—typically sacrificing your desires and priorities as a way to avoid conflict or disapproval, you may decide to pick the movie *you* want to watch rather than acquiescing to your partner's preference once again. Your usual pattern of putting yourself last is likely a self-protective habit that actually *undermines* equality, breeds resentment and contempt, and restricts the potential for genuine connection. If this resonates for you, assertively putting yourself first more often will likely help your relationship long term.

Remember, there *is* no relationship or connection without both of you, just as there is no butterfly without two equally strong sets of wings. Whether you want to be happier or you want your partner to be happier, you're both equally important. By considering yourself (if you tend not to), you're not being selfish, you're helping your relationship flourish by becoming the best you can be. What makes you stronger as one of the sets of wings simultaneously makes the butterfly stronger, as long as there's balance between the two of you over time. Just as each wing's strength is vital for the butterfly's flight, your individual growth uplifts and propels the entire relationship forward, creating a harmonious and dynamic synergy.

Interdependence or mutual reliance requires a person to have the capacity to be both independent and dependent, to lead and to follow, to go first and to go last, at different times in various circumstances. Discerning what will benefit the connection between you and your partner at any given moment is the key. This is the shift in mindset or the transformation of motivation: aiming yourself toward the *benefit of the connection* between you and your partner, rather than only toward yourself at your partner's expense or only toward your partner at your own expense. If you're asking yourself, *How can I help us connect?* you're on the right track.

Understanding the transformation of motivation is crucial in grasping how successful couples manage conflict, make sacrifices, and strengthen their bond. It suggests the most satisfying and stable partnerships are those in which *both* individuals consistently consider and prioritize the well-being of their union above self and other. Recognizing that each partner is an integral component of the partnership, the aim is to foster inclusivity. Both partners should direct their efforts toward nurturing the connection that binds them, much like caring for the body of a butterfly. This shared commitment ensures that the relationship itself becomes the focal point of their collective journey.

The concept of the transformation of motivation finds echoes in various religious teachings, such as Christianity, Judaism, Islam, and Buddhism. In Christianity, it mirrors the teachings of Jesus about loving one's neighbor and the communal sharing of the Last Supper. In Judaism, it aligns with the concept of Tikkun Olam, repairing the world through acts of kindness. Islamic teachings also reflect this concept in the communal spirit and empathy encouraged among the Ummah, or global Muslim community. Similarly, in Buddhism, it resonates with the idea of interconnectedness and compassion in the Noble Eightfold Path. In each of these belief systems (and countless other religious traditions), the transformation from self-focused motives to prioritizing the collective well-being resonates with the core principles of establishing and maintaining meaningful, harmonious relationships.

Poets and philosophers have always understood this truth about relationships as we see from the following quotes:

"Love is composed of a single soul inhabiting two bodies."
– Aristotle

"Let there be spaces in your togetherness, and let the winds of the heavens dance between you. Love one another but make not a bond of love: Let it be rather a moving sea between the shores of your souls."
– Khalil Gibran

The modern American poet Robert Bly comes closest to describing what is going on in healthy relationships. In his poem "The Third Body," he describes the relationship as an entity the couple cares for, something that emerges between them when they join forces—like a baby. The relationship is an entirely new being that has its own needs, wants, and desires. Bly expresses

They obey a third body that they share in common.
They have made a promise to love that body.

The *third body* Bly describes is a shared space, an in-betweenness, that connects two people in a relationship. This place literally *is* the energy the two partners create synergistically together through the love they invest. The third entity in Bly's poem stabilizes the connection because the two partners "love that body."

The Butterfly Blueprint offers a visual representation of interdependence for romantic relationships. The body of the butterfly—in between the two sets of wings—is the shared space, just like the overlapping area between the two circles in a Venn diagram. If one circle was blue and the other red, the overlapping area would be purple—a combination or intermingling of the two, a new color—new life.

That is, the "body" or connection is not merely the sum of the two parts but rather a magical *new* entity comes into being through effective interdependence.

Partner A   "We"   Partner B

The two sets of wings are interdependent. They rely on one another and also have an identity of their own.

While couples and families are foundational to human society and the world at large, research consistently illuminates a somber reality: About half of first marriages end in divorce, two thirds of second marriages, and three-quarters of third marriages. According to the Holmes and Rahe Stress Scale, the distress inherent in divorce is only trumped by the death of a spouse, and the ripple effects extend to the youngest members of the family.

Children from divorced families face their own set of challenges, including emotional struggles, academic and behavioral issues, social trouble, adjustment to new family structures, and economic hardship. Research also indicates that children whose parents divorce are more likely to experience divorce themselves as adults.

In our rapidly evolving society, mere survival or coexistence isn't the end goal most couples seek. We don't want to feel like business partners, roommates, or co-parents. We don't want to just stay together. We want fulfillment. We yearn for that spark or chemistry, for our hearts to flutter with vitality. We want to thrive together long term.

Much like the allegory of the long spoons, the space between you can be a heaven or a hell, a safe haven or a battleground. By adopting an attitude of interdependence, cooperation, and mutual respect, you will generate new energy that benefits both of you. The true essence of a relationship, much like the flight of a butterfly, isn't found solely in the strength of each individual or set of wings, but in the harmonious interaction *between* them.

The Butterfly Blueprint does more than just point you in the right direction—it provides you with practical tools and actionable practices. By embracing the eight principles in this guide, your relationship can successfully transition through its metamorphosis and eventually flourish. Like a caterpillar transforming into a beautiful butterfly, your partnership can be rejuvenated, allowing both of you to become your very best selves in the process—whole and intimate, together.

Part Two consists of eight chapters, each detailing a unique principle of interdependent relationships. Central to these principles is the concept of a "transformation of motivation"—a pivotal shift from being entangled in various "duality dilemmas" to deliberately and consciously focusing on the mutual benefit of the partnership. This shift emphasizes the importance of nurturing the shared connection, symbolized as the body of the butterfly, representing the single heart of the couple bond. Each chapter also offers three practical strategies to implement the principle, giving clear answers to the question, *"What should we do?"*

So, are you ready to do your inner work? Are you prepared to empower your relationship with the wings it deserves? If so, let's dive into the Butterfly Blueprint together! Let your love story take flight!

5

Surrender

"The creative process is a process of surrender, not control."
– Julia Cameron

One sunny summer day, my husband, Matthew, and I were on a 55-kilometer bike ride. Road biking is our favorite hobby to do together. We enjoy the breeze, the downhill thrill, and feeling strong. Once in a while, we have a friendly race, even though we both know who will win.

We stopped at the side of the road to have a short drink break when I casually asked Matthew what he thought about the "honey-do" list I had given him a few days earlier. It was the first such list I had ever given him over the 13-year span of our relationship. We were both going to be off of work the following week, and Matthew tended to get busy with household projects on his own initiative, so I figured I might as well let him know what jobs were on my radar as well.

"I'm not interested in your list; I'm not your slave" was his snappy response.

I was shocked and caught off guard. I cut the break short as I blurted out, "I guess I'll have to hire someone." And, off I went.

The mood turned cold and distant as we both kept to ourselves for the rest of the ride. We were each tangled up in our own root systems, not really seeing the other, projecting our underdeveloped shadow parts onto one another, and I was telling myself lots and lots of stories, trying to make sense of things.

I never said you were my slave, I argued silently in my mind. *I have never thought of you as my slave. How could you think I see you that way? I don't even give you 'honey-do' lists. I've never had to ask you to do anything because you're always on top of all the renos and fix-it jobs.*

My growing internal defense continued: *If he feels this way, I must have made him feel that, right? He thinks I'm the bad guy! But I can't be the bad guy because I don't even see him as a slave in the first place!*

Later that day, Matthew was watching TV in our open-concept space that includes the kitchen, dining room, and living room as I continued silently with the stories in my head. I was washing a fresh flat of strawberries in the kitchen, getting them ready to freeze, as my inner narrative charged ahead: *I didn't do anything wrong. I'm not the slave-driver he's making me out to be! I'm a good wife! I'm a nice person! How could he see me in such a negative way?! He shouldn't have snapped at me! I didn't deserve that!*

"You know you triggered yourself, right?! I have never thought of you as my slave. You're just telling yourself stories about me!" I snapped, not able to contain it any longer.

Matthew quickly shot back, "I wouldn't have felt like a slave if you didn't give me the list! You're telling yourself stories too! I never said you were the bad guy! I don't know why you're saying that!"

My anger seeped through in my sarcastic tone as I pushed back: "Okay, I promise I won't ever tell you my desires or wishes, or communicate my likes and dislikes with you ever again, period!"

A flood of sensations and emotions swirled through my body. I was hurt. I was mad. I felt misunderstood and helpless. I wanted to scream or give up. I wanted to disappear. I felt desperate. Normally, I yell and call Matthew names if I can't get through to him in a calm way. Somewhere inside of me, I would feel justified in trying to hurt him or shock him into hearing me and empathizing with me. But all of the reactivity just causes a downward spiral and leads us straight to a dead end, every time.

It was at that moment that something of a miracle happened. I paused within myself just long enough to realize I had options. I could choose how to respond rather than just allowing my nervous system to have free reign and react however it wanted. It was a moment in which I experienced a flash of free choice. I felt myself switch gears inside and I surrendered.

I decided to take a different approach and do a U-turn (or "you-turn" toward Matthew's perspective). In that brief pause, I was able to put "we" above "me" and aimed to repair the connection between us. I thought to myself, *Why should our whole day be ruined over something so unimportant?* I physically approached Matthew, put my hand on his shoulder, and said, "Sweetheart, I'm sorry I made you feel like a slave, and you're right: I'm telling myself stories as well. I'm telling myself you think I'm the bad guy. You're right."

"Yeah—I'm not a child and I don't need lists. I don't like lists. I can see what needs to be done myself," Matthew quickly uttered.

"I'm on your side, Matthew," I reassured him.

"You can just tell me if you want something done. You don't need to give me a list. It just hangs over my head and makes me feel pressured, like I have a timeline to get it done," he continued with an edge.

"I understand," I replied. Then, something quickly switched back inside of me and I decided to press *my* perspective once again. "My feelings are hurt by the way you're talking to me—the energy—it hurts me," I added as softly as I could and held my breath.

Then, another miracle happened. Instead of walking away and shutting down like usual, Matthew looked at me, directly in my eyes, and said, "I'm sorry your feelings got hurt." He said it again, adding my name: "I'm sorry your feelings got hurt, Amanda."

His acknowledgment of my feelings and use of my name felt like soothing, cool water on the sparks that had been rapidly becoming flames between us. I quickly, almost in a whisper, said, "Thank you."

I went back to washing my strawberries and showed Matthew one that looked like a penis, hairy balls and all. We shared a giggle and continued on with our day, the emotional bond between us having been repaired through mutual surrender. From that place of surrender, I was able to see Matthew and he was able to hear me. We were able to be inclusive of each other again. The reactive, stormy space between us had been restored into a calm, connected, peaceful place.

* * *

The first foundational principle of the Butterfly Blueprint is *surrender*. Envision a leaf on the water's surface, guided effortlessly by the gentle flow of the stream. The leaf doesn't resist, fight against the current, or force another path. It simply allows the water to carry it. This is the essence of surrender—letting go of any resistance and allowing the course of events to unfold naturally, minus the ego's agenda, which is always working on behalf of the self *alone* (even if unconsciously in the world of roots).

The caterpillar provides us with a stellar example of surrender. At a certain juncture in its life, too bloated from the consumption of leaves to go on, it instinctively recognizes the need to undergo a metamorphic transformation. Instead of clinging to what is familiar and comfortable, it surrenders by hanging itself upside down and wrapping itself into a chrysalis.

Within this chrysalis, the pupa stage unfolds in stillness, marking a time of profound internal change. The immature caterpillar reorganizes its structure and physiology to emerge as a mature adult insect.

The caterpillar trusts this process implicitly, even though it means leaving behind all that it once was, to embrace a new, uncharted future. This profound letting-go is essential for its eventual rebirth as a butterfly. Surrender is brave. It's also necessary if we want a better outcome.

"What the caterpillar calls the end, the rest of the world calls a butterfly."
– Richard Bach

Surrender means placing trust in love's natural evolution. It's about releasing control, embracing uncertainty, and letting the relationship develop organically. In essence, we get out of our own way, thereby making room for love to enter the space between us.

By surrendering, partners acknowledge they don't have all the answers or a constructive way forward. With a do-no-harm attitude, they carve out a space between them, making room for something different, something better. By surrendering, they consciously build the overlapping circle area of the Venn diagram—the body of the butterfly that connects the two sets of wings.

Each partner pauses, birthing new time and space between them—a new entity that wasn't there before—the "new body" from Robert Bly's poem in the introduction to Part Two. Neither pollutes (with complaints and criticism) or neglects this space. They both allow it to come into being between them, creating the potential for it to transform from an *empty space* into a *sacred place* as they continue on their journey through the eight principles of the Butterfly Blueprint.

Surrender is blocked as long as we are caught up in the *attack-defend* duality dilemma. It's a duality dilemma because you can't know one—attack—without the other—defend—just like you can't have a coin without its two sides; they are inseparable. So, when we engage in one—let's say attack—we inevitably invite the other—defense—and like a tug-of-war, the more one attacks, the more the other defends, and the more the other defends, the more the first one attacks.

In this cycle of conflict, roles blur as the victim and perpetrator switch places, making it hard to tell them apart as the argument spirals. Victim and perpetrator are two sides of yet another coin: conflict, which is inevitable since the overlapping circle area in the Venn diagram or the body of the butterfly is shared. Conflict is inherent to life with its infinite duality dilemmas. It's no longer about "who started it," since both partners fuel the conflict through their reactions. Things snowball as the argument heads downhill. Like struggling to get out of quicksand, the couple sinks deeper and faster with every mindless reaction.

Matthew and I were caught up in the attack-defend duality dilemma in the biking story that opened this chapter: "You know you triggered yourself, right?! I have never thought of you as my slave. You're just telling yourself stories about me!" That was my attack. "I wouldn't have felt like a slave if you didn't give me the list! You're telling yourself stories too! I never said you were the bad guy! I don't know why you're saying that!" That was Matthew's defense.

At the core of this pattern is the brain's amygdala. This tiny structure plays a pivotal role in processing emotions, especially those linked to our survival instincts, which are often triggered when we experience emotional disconnection from our partners. When the amygdala becomes overly activated, it can lead to what's known as an "amygdala hijack" when a person "flips their lid." This reflexive reaction drives us into modes of fight, flight, or freeze (and fix), as the frontal cortex is blocked from functioning and the survival brain kicks into high gear. We lose the pause between thought and action. We just act or, more accurately, we just *react!*

The fight, flight, and freeze stress responses are instinctive physiological reactions to perceived threats. The fight response—a readiness for confrontation—can show up as lashing out, blaming, demanding, or criticizing. The flight response—a desire to escape the situation—might manifest as avoiding or distancing oneself from one's partner. The freeze response—like a deer in the headlights—shows up as overwhelm, emotional shutdown, or numbness.

In her book *Hold Me Tight* (2008), Dr. Sue Johnson describes "demon dialogues," which are destructive communication patterns in relationships, driven by fight, flight, and freeze responses. These include "Find the Bad Guy," a blame game cycle with no resolution; "The Protest Polka," where one partner aggressively seeks connection while the other withdraws; and "Freeze and Flee," where both partners emotionally shut down and are backed into the separate corners of "you" and "me," leading to a cold impasse with little conflict but also minimal connection.

In *The Break-Up* movie, a seemingly minor incident—Gary (Vince Vaughn) not helping with the dishes after a dinner party—sparks a significant argument with Brooke (Jennifer Aniston). This fight quickly reveals the deeper rifts in their relationship. Brooke seeks a more emotionally engaged connection with Gary but fails to convey her need effectively. Her frustrations pour out in a series of complaints, from Gary's failure to buy enough lemons to his reluctance to attend the ballet, culminating in her exasperated declaration, "I want you to *want* to do the dishes!" Meanwhile, Gary, preoccupied with his video games, is perplexed and annoyed, unable to grasp the deeper emotional context behind Brooke's grievances. The scene poignantly illustrates how trivial domestic squabbles often mask profound emotional disconnection and longing.

Imagine a butterfly with each of its wings pulling in opposite directions, or one set of wings attacking the other while the second set tries to escape. Instead of fluttering gracefully, there's a lack of coordination and wasted energy. The body of the butterfly would be confused and overwhelmed, caught between the two warring parties. The two pairs of wings would be working against the very source of their own sustenance: the connection between them.

Similarly, when you lash out or avoid your partner, you inadvertently damage the relationship and, by extension, yourself. This is because your personal well-being is intertwined with the connection you share. The shared space between you, like the overlapping area in a Venn diagram, suffers under the strain of attack-defense dynamics. A power struggle consumes this shared territory, and it's ultimately abandoned as both partners retreat to their separate corners—the outlier areas on the Venn diagram. The potential for effective interdependence is destroyed.

To truly change the cycle of conflict and disconnection, both partners must find the courage to surrender, which is not about submission, giving in, or admitting defeat. It's about letting go of repetitive, ineffective behaviors and embarking on a new path. Surrender makes more room for human *being* in the place of human *doing*. By stepping away from the habitual fight and choosing something different, you give your "butterfly" a chance to heal and fly again. There are three key practices to help you master the principle of surrender: being defenseless, present, and open.

The first practice in attaining the principle of surrender is to *be defenseless*. This might sound dangerous, naïve, and maybe even foolish. Why would anyone want to render themselves exposed and vulnerable? Don't forget, the emotional and physical connection you share with your partner *is* your main source of protection and security. By embracing a posture of defenselessness, you are shifting from self-protection to connection-protection, and you benefit from connection-protection just as much as your partner does. This is the difference! By protecting the connection, you're caring for *both* yourself *and* your partner, rather than only one at the expense of the other.

Being defenseless means setting aside the metaphorical weapons including hurtful words, emotional walls, and the self-defeating, kneejerk fight, flight, and freeze stress reactions: attack, defend, and shut down. It means stopping actions that clearly don't work and, in fact, make things worse. This requires relinquishing control—the need to always be right, to win every argument, to have the last word, or to uphold an image of perfection.

In his book *The New Rules of Marriage* (2007), Terrence Real, renowned family therapist, highlights various forms of psychological abuse or relational violence that need to cease unconditionally. These damaging behaviors include actions that violate a person's psychological boundaries such as yelling, screaming, name-calling, shaming, humiliating, ridiculing, and mocking. Additionally, harmful tactics like sarcasm, condescending humor, patronizing attitudes, dictating what an adult should think or feel, telling your partner what he or she "really" thinks or feels, making and breaking promises, lying, manipulating, and controlling behaviors all contribute to a toxic environment.

If abuse and care are considered two sides of yet another coin, then the coin itself would be relationship or human interaction. The coin represents the spectrum of ways in which individuals relate to and treat each other in relationships of all sorts. Human interactions encompass the full range of positive to negative behaviors and dynamics, with nurturance representing the supportive, caring, and uplifting side, and abuse embodying the harmful, destructive, and diminishing side. The coin underscores the potential within all relationships to foster growth and wellbeing or cause harm and suffering.

Being defenseless doesn't mean you don't take action to protect yourself from abuse. Being defenseless doesn't mean you agree with your partner, become a pushover, lose, or cancel your own position. It doesn't mean you don't exercise thoughtful, supple boundaries in a conscious manner. It means that you stop doing harm and making things worse by restraining yourself from the impulse to lash out.

It means the action you take will be consciously thought through and chosen rather than based upon ingrained defense mechanisms from childhood that get you caught up in cyclical arguments that go nowhere. It means that, were you to watch a replay of the scenario on videotape, you wouldn't feel ashamed of your behavior or regret it. It means that if there were witnesses present, such as some of your co-workers, you would act in the same manner.

Defenselessness fosters trust in the shared space between you and your partner. It paves the way for deeper understanding and a stronger, more resilient bond. It means embracing the truth, the reality of duality: you're in it together, just like the two sides of a coin.

Reflect on your reactions during tense moments with your partner. Do you engage in the fight, flight, freeze, or fix stress responses? All of the above at different times? How do you show up during fights? What words tumble out? How does your body feel? Picture yourself watching a disagreement with your partner on video. What stands out? What do you hear yourself say? What do you see yourself do?

I often ask couples, "If I was a fly on the wall at your place when you're having an argument, what would I experience? Paint a picture for me so I can be there with you." You can imagine that you are that fly on the wall, watching yourself from the side. What if your co-workers were present, how would your behavior change? Focus on your *own* behavior, *not* your partner's. Write down all your destructive defensive maneuvers. Self-awareness is key in moving forward constructively.

If raising your voice or yelling is your go-to move, deliberately work to be aware of it and do your best to maintain an even tone during disagreements. If specific words act as your shield, note them. What are the hurtful phrases you utter and later regret? Do you passive-aggressively punish your partner by leaving or shutting down? Make a concerted effort to recognize and curb your knee-jerk defenses.

Rate how out-of-control you feel when your fight, flight, freeze stress reactions take over on a scale from 1 to 10, with 10 indicating maximum distress and 1 being minimum. Strive to reduce their potency. If yelling ranks at a 9, aim to bring it down to an 8, then a 7, and continue until it's below 5. If checking out and shutting down is your go-to move, focus on bringing it down a few notches on the scale. Afterward, tackle the next defense that rates closest to 10. Keep practicing, one baby step at a time.

The second practice on your way to attaining the principle of surrender is to *be present*. Imagine you're a radio, and every day, you scan through a multitude of stations, your focus switching from one thing to another as you move throughout your day. Each station represents your thoughts, observations, worries, intentions, and plans.

Practicing presence means tuning into a single station—your partner's experience—and listening intently, without interference or static from all the other channels. Your focus isn't disturbed. Rather, you are absorbed by your partner's experience, leaning into it with all five senses. *What would it be like to be in my partner's shoes right now?* you wonder. You're shining a spotlight on your partner, letting them bask in your undivided attention. This communicates they are valued, cherished, and worthy of your time.

In a relationship, presence occurs in the overlapping area of a Venn diagram, where you lean into your partner's circle as much as possible without demanding, intruding, or pushing. It involves repositioning the center point from the middle of your own circle to its edge, bringing you closer to your partner's experience, placing the center point in the shared space between you. It's about showing up physically and emotionally for your partner. It's as if you're looking through a window into your partner's world—more than just physical proximity, it's an expansion of your perception, a deliberate attempt to understand your partner's unique experience, to be in *their* body and feel the world through *their* five senses, even making efforts to feel into their roots.

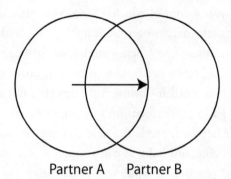

Partner A   Partner B

The arrow shows how partner A is mindfully leaning into
the experience of partner B with all five senses as much as possible.

Often equated with *mindfulness* or *attunement*, being present is vital for the health and success of couple relationships. Research done by Doctors John and Jane Gottman show that "turning toward" your partner plays a significant role in relationship satisfaction and longevity, especially when your partner shows "bids for connection" (2006, pg. 5–6). If your partner asks you, "How was your day?" this is a "bid for connection" and an opportunity to practice presence by leaning in and sharing a bonding moment. Presence embodies awareness, noting nonverbal details such as the sparkle in your partner's eyes when excited or a brief sigh when worried.

Picture, for a moment, an activity or a person you enjoy—be it a World Cup soccer match, the meticulous craft of baking your favorite cake, or watching your beloved child sleep. Think about how you immerse yourself in those moments or activities, giving your full, undivided attention. You might be so enthralled that time seems to stand still.

When we are internally rewarded, we are willing to give generously of our time, attention, energy, and effort. We invest ourselves and are willing to make efforts, perhaps taking courses to refine a skill or memorizing the names of every player on our favorite team. Every detail matters because we enjoy it, engaging not just our hearts but our minds and all our strength as well.

Now, with that level of engagement in mind, consider how you might bring the same depth of presence and motivation into your relationship with your partner. Take a moment to look at your partner. What do you see? Look into your partner's eyes. What might you have missed? Listen to your partner. What's the heart of what they're really trying to say? Is there some truth in their message, even if it's only partial? What is their body language communicating? Try to feel into your partner's branches and even their roots with everything you have, in a non-demanding, non-intrusive way.

In the heat of the moment, make efforts to feel beyond your partner's defense mechanisms to the core of their experience. This isn't merely about being physically present, but about delving into the emotional connection you share with your partner. You can practice this during conversation as well as periods of silence.

Presence is more about *being* than *doing* and more internal than corporeal. In order to give your full attention to your partner, you will need to limit distractions and be still. Sit or stand in one place. Put your phone down. Turn the TV off. Look up from your computer and turn your posture so your torso is facing your partner. Tell your kids they will have to wait a few minutes if they interrupt.

Be aware of any urge or instinct to interrupt or "correct" what your partner is saying or doing, or to try to fix things for your partner by offering solutions, suggestions, and unsolicited advice. The power of just *being there*, sharing in your partner's experience and showing care, cannot be overstated. Being present in the present is the greatest present you can give your partner. You are the present! Usually, being fully there is the only "fix" your partner really needs or wants.

The third key practice in attaining the principle of surrender is to *be open*. Imagine you're a book. Over time, pages might become stuck together and certain chapters might be more challenging to access. To be open is to do your best to let your partner in.

Being open in a relationship is like taking a few bricks out of the wall of your circle in a Venn diagram. It's like consciously opening the curtains on the windows of your heart and mind, inviting your partner to step into your internal world of roots. Since your partner cannot perceive your roots through their five senses, the only way for them to truly be there with you in that space is if you welcome them in.

This can be scary for sure. Who knows what could be found there in that messy, dark place inside you. Who knows what could happen once you've said something that only you knew before. It could be used against you. It's risky but it's riskier to keep your partner as an outsider, not knowing how you feel or what you desire, fumbling in the dark, trying to get it right without any help.

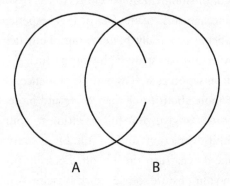

The opening shows how partner A is letting partner B in.

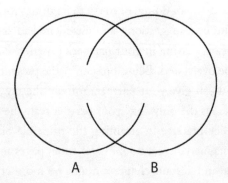

When both partners let each other in, they make an opening for connection, for the body of the butterfly.

Many clients in couples' counseling express a longing to be "let in." Your partner may be standing in the overlapping area of your Venn diagram, the place that is supposed to be shared, *waiting* for you, yearning for a connection that can only happen when two people are present in that place together at the same time.

You don't have to be perfect and show up without blemishes or flaws. Just show up! Be yourself. Openness—a willingness to be vulnerable—gives your partner the message you trust them and feel safe with them, at least safe enough to take the risk of letting them in. The transparency of openness fosters the potential for deeper connection and emotional (and even physical) intimacy.

Many of us were taught to maintain a cheerful façade and keep emotions private in childhood. Boys, especially, were told, "Never let them see you cry." Girls were taught to keep their anger (and assertiveness) in. Expressing anger in an assertive way or shedding tears are often met with disapproval, pushing us into emotional isolation. We end up fearing rejection and abandonment which can feel even more painful than staying guarded. However, true intimacy emerges from sharing your authentic self, even when it's challenging. You can either stay closed, protected, and alone or risk being open, vulnerable, and connected.

Navigating one's internal landscape or "mindscape" as Dan Siegel calls it, isn't second nature for everyone (2017). Many people grow up without acknowledgment (from their caregivers) that the world of roots even exists, never mind encouragement to explore or express feelings. Most people didn't have good role models for communication.

Many clients shyly confess, "I'm not very articulate. My partner is so much better with feelings. I need to find the right words before I share. I like to process things on my own, in my head." And you know what? That's perfectly okay. It doesn't make you inferior. How could you know if you were never shown? We need all kinds of people in this world! You excel at many other things! Understand that openness, like any skill, requires time and practice. Think of it as learning a new language. With patience and commitment, you can master it, one word or gesture at a time.

Janet Hurley's Feedback Wheel encourages clear, concise, honest communication and helps individuals express their feelings and needs effectively. It consists of four steps:

1. **What you saw or heard:** Begin with factual observations without assumptions, such as "When I said good morning, you walked away."

2. **What you made up about it:** Share your interpretation or the story you told yourself about the observation, for example, "I told myself that you were upset with me."

3. **How it made you feel:** Express your emotions related to the situation by saying, for instance, "I felt sad and angry."

4. **What you would like moving forward:** State your preferred response for future interactions, such as "I'd prefer to be acknowledged when I say good morning."

To truly foster openness in your relationship, approach it with the same curiosity and patience as mastering any new skill or hobby. Just as you allow yourself grace to fumble and learn when taking on a new job or craft, give yourself the same latitude as you learn to articulate yourself and be more open. Embrace the learning curve and understand that mistakes or misunderstandings are just stepping stones toward success. No one gets it right every time, and you can always repair if things go south.

Dare to let down your guard. Take the risk of letting your partner in, not as a flawless entity but as the evolving person you are. It's through this shared openness that relationships find their richest depths. As Brené Brown wrote in *Daring Greatly* (2012), vulnerability is not about victory or defeat, since we need both. It's about engaging.

In order to deepen your bond, start by taking a small step toward unveiling your inner self. Consider sharing something new about yourself with your partner—perhaps a fleeting thought, a modest dream, or a mild concern. Choose something that feels manageable, ranking around a "4" on your personal vulnerability scale (where "10" is deeply revealing). Initiate this act of trust and watch your partner's reaction. Was the outcome as daunting as you had anticipated? By changing your approach, you receive different feedback, which might then persuade you that opening up *can* be safe and rewarding. It might not be as bad as you thought. Perhaps your fears are rooted in the past and no longer apply. True interdependent connection is just beyond the risk, waiting for you to gather the courage to invite your partner in.

* * *

James and Linda are a happily married couple who have decided to take on a do-it-yourself kitchen renovation. While they share a love for their home, their differing approaches toward this project are creating conflict.

James, who is generally more impulsive, prefers to dive head-first into tasks. He finds joy in the process of figuring things out as he goes along, which gives him a sense of adventure. To him, the kitchen renovation is an exciting challenge to be conquered hands-on, with power tools ablaze.

On the other hand, Linda prefers a methodical and well-planned approach to projects and tasks. She believes in reading the instruction manual, researching best practices, and following a step-by-step plan to ensure that no detail is overlooked and the project is completed correctly the first time.

Their differences have caused a few tense moments. James feels stifled and micromanaged when Linda insists on discussing every detail. He starts to question whether Linda trusts his capabilities and judgment. He feels that her constant desire to control the process diminishes his role and the value he can bring to the project.

Meanwhile, Linda feels stressed and frustrated with James's impromptu approach. She worries that his hurried attitude to getting things done will lead to mistakes, and these mistakes might end up costing them more time, money, and effort in the long run.

They both understand they need to find a balance between their two styles, but how to get there remains a conundrum. James and Linda's divergent approaches to their project are a perfect storm just waiting to happen.

Fortunately, James and Linda have been trying to incorporate the Butterfly Blueprint practices into their relationship. They venture into this renovation project, aiming to surrender in three key ways: practicing being defenseless, present, and open. As they stand in their half-finished kitchen, surrounded by blueprints, toolboxes, and an air of tension, James and Linda manage not to get stuck as they talk:

James feels stifled and, with his hands on his hips, blurts out, "Linda, I feel like you're trying to micromanage everything. It's like you don't trust that I know what I'm doing."

"That's not true, James," Linda responds with a stressed tone, her hands nervously clutching the blueprint. "It's not about trust. I just don't want us to make mistakes we'll regret."

James takes a deep breath, recognizing his impulsive need to dive right in could be causing Linda distress. "Okay, I get it." he says, trying to stay calm and remembering the need to be defenseless. "You're just trying to avoid unnecessary complications and setbacks." James focuses on being present and open as he adds, "But I also need *you* to understand that my way of doing things isn't wrong. It's just different from yours."

Linda looks at him, appreciating his openness and seeing an opportunity for deeper connection. She makes a conscious effort to soften her approach, surrendering her need to control every detail and states, "You're right, James. Your approach isn't wrong, and

I'm sorry if I made you feel that way. We're in this together, and we need to respect each other's methods. What's that called again? Equifinality! There are many ways to reach the goal!"

Linda steps closer, puts the blueprints down, and extends her hands toward James in an act of surrender and openness. "Let's do this together. We can make a rough plan, and as we progress, we'll tweak things as necessary. Does that work?" she asks, committed to maintaining the delicate emotional balance between them.

James smiles, appreciating her effort to merge their approaches. He feels acknowledged, valued, and reassured as he responds, "Yes, that sounds fair. Let's do this together. It's our project, after all. It's our home."

Surrender: A Reflective Exercise for Couples

It's time for some relationship archaeology! You're going to dig up a recent relationship "win" and inspect it under the light of the Butterfly Blueprint.

Think back to a time you both successfully resolved a disagreement, a time when the dust of the dispute settled and you both felt pretty good about how things turned out. Now, grab your magnifying glass because we're going on a treasure hunt for elements of surrender!

Even though you might not have realized it then, one or both of you probably practiced principle number one of the Butterfly Blueprint: surrender. Upon reflection, did you notice either of you were trying to be defenseless? Were there moments when you put down your emotional weapons and thought twice before reacting?

What about being present? Can you recall if either of you were fully there, emotionally and mentally, during the resolution? Were your minds and hearts fully engaged in the conversation? Were you leaning in toward your partner's experience?

And finally, let's look at the role of being open. Did you find yourself being transparent about your feelings and thoughts even if they were difficult to express? Were you willing to let your partner in? Did you try to open your heart?

Reflect on these questions individually, then come together to discuss your findings. Discuss how the three practices—being defenseless, present, and open—played into your successful resolution. You might be surprised to find you were practicing the first principle of the Butterfly Blueprint—surrender—without knowing it at the time!

This exercise is not just about understanding the past but about paving the way for resolving future disagreements. By understanding how surrender worked for you in the past, you'll be better equipped to navigate future challenges more consciously. Remember, every disagreement is an opportunity for surrender, growth, and deeper connection.

6

Equality

"No one can make you feel inferior without your consent."
– Eleanor Roosevelt

George Clooney was at the height of his bachelor status, a Hollywood heartthrob and renowned playboy. The media loved to speculate about his romantic interests, especially when A-list actresses like Julia Roberts, Sandra Bullock, and Charlize Theron were thrown into the mix. People couldn't help but wonder who he would eventually settle down with—or if he would even marry at all. The suspense was enough to make the fainthearted swoon.

Then, on April 28, 2014, the headlines shocked the world. George Clooney was engaged. But "Who on earth is Amal?!" was the question on everyone's lips. She wasn't a Hollywood star, and financially, her wealth was dwarfed by George's. From a celebrity perspective, she didn't appear to be his equal. The gossip mill was in full swing, wondering how these two had met and how they would manage.

The media played up the disparity between George and Amal, suggesting that he could have had anyone—someone as famous, someone as rich. They could have been the ultimate power couple in Hollywood. Yet, amid all the teasing, a beautiful truth emerged.

Amal Alamuddin was a highly accomplished human rights lawyer, working on important international cases. While she may not have had George's fame, she possessed a depth of knowledge and passion for her work that truly impressed him. As their relationship blossomed, it became evident she was more than just an intellectual match for George; she was a heavyweight in her own right.

Amal's legal expertise and dedication to making a difference in the world had a profound impact on George. She broadened his worldview and inspired him to be more involved in humanitarian causes, leveraging his fame and fortune for good. But it wasn't just about her impressive career. Amal's grounded nature and life outside of Hollywood brought balance into George's life. She kept him rooted, and he brought joy and laughter into her life, easing the pressures of her high-stakes profession.

Their relationship is built on mutual respect and appreciation for each other's contributions. Despite the differences in their public profiles, they see each other as equals, valuing the unique strengths they each bring to the table. Neither is superior or inferior. They recognize equality is not about matching fame or fortune; it is about recognizing the value each person brings to the relationship.

* * *

Equality is the second principle of the Butterfly Blueprint. True equality in a relationship is about supporting each other's passions and goals—no matter how different they may be—in a balanced way. It's about recognizing and valuing the individual worth of each partner, appreciating unique strengths, and building a partnership that thrives on mutual respect and admiration.

The two set of wings on a butterfly are equal even though they oppose one another; they work in tandem to achieve flight. In fact, it is precisely because the sets of wings oppose and complement one another that a butterfly can flutter from summer lilac to lilac. And, just as a butterfly cannot fly with only one set of wings, or one big set and one little set, a couple cannot thrive if one partner is considered to be less or more worthy than the other. Both sets of wings, like both partners, are integral to the effective interdependent functioning of the whole. They are equally valuable.

Picture a set of scales, perfectly balanced, with neither side tipping lower or higher than the other. This equilibrium is a visual representation of equality, where both sides are given equal weight, importance, and value, ensuring harmony. In communities, equality stands as a pillar of fairness and justice. It's not about identical sameness or fifty-fifty-ness, which are unrealistic and impossible to achieve. It means every diverse individual is valued equally as an integral part of the whole.

Navigating equality is hard to do because imbalances *do* constantly show up. One carries the stress of the mental load. One makes more money. One does more housework. One parents more. One has a physical or mental health issue and the other picks up the slack. These discrepancies beg the question, how do we embrace equality when it's impossible to measure or compare the value of folding laundry with the value of driving the kids to soccer? Or the value of taking care of an aging mother-in-law in contrast to the value of getting a promotion at work?

It's crucial to consistently evaluate and reflect: Does a particular choice or focus foster equality or inequality between you and your partner in the long run? Balancing your roles, how you spend your time, and what you put money and effort into is indeed an art— one that demands thoughtful consideration. How do you value the principle of equality when it comes to the decisions you make about where you invest yourself?

Picture yourself and your partner as the two sets of wings on a butterfly. There are moments when nurturing your individual set of wings—your personal growth and well-being—is best for the connection you share. Other times, it will be incumbent upon you to support your partner's wings, setting your own needs aside. How do you discern how balanced things are and what needs to happen to build more balance so that you and your partner feel equally valuable at the end of the day?

The undercurrents of the *dominance-submission* duality dilemma persistently try to nudge one partner above or below the other in value, undermining equality in a relationship. This duality, deeply embedded in the human psyche and our social conditioning, can unconsciously infiltrate a relationship, leading couples to act out the opposing positions. While dominance may manifest as overt or covert control or decision-making power, submission can appear as passive acceptance or the suppression of one's own needs and desires.

In the realm of interpersonal dynamics, surrender and submission may sound similar, but they carry distinct meanings and connotations. Surrender, as explored in Chapter Five, is seen as a willful and conscious act of letting go, releasing the need for control. It's a voluntary process, grounded in understanding for a greater good. For example, someone might surrender to a higher power, a universal flow, or even unpredictability in life. This act is empowering, as it is rooted in the recognition of one's boundaries and the choice to embrace the expansiveness of an experience, a moment, or a relationship.

Submission, on the other hand, implies a more passive acquiescence or yielding to force or authority. It's often associated with obedience or compliance, sometimes even under duress. Submission can be a result of external pressure or an internal belief that one is lesser, undeserving, or inadequate. While there are contexts where submission is chosen freely and is not negative (like in certain cultural, spiritual, or even playful scenarios), in many instances, it denotes a power imbalance that blocks connection.

Historically, societal norms, cultural expectations, and even religious beliefs have tended to favor placing the more masculine partner in a dominant position. However, true harmony isn't about designating roles or assigning false positions of power based on sex, gender, or any other identifying characteristic. The age-old tussle between dominance and submission isn't about determining who's on top, but about understanding that genuine interdependent partnership requires equal worth and value. It makes sense that if one partner is good with money, they will lead in that area, but this does not involve domination or submission if both partners agree.

The dominance-submission duality dilemma manifests powerfully in codependent dynamics. In contrast to interdependence, where both partners maintain their unique, independent identities while engaging in mutual reliance, codependence is characterized by an *excessive* dependence on one's partner for validation, approval, and a sense of identity (Beattie, 2022). This leads to power imbalances where partners may alternately find themselves in roles of dominance or submission, depending on the context and circumstances. Over time, the relationship often oscillates between these two extremes, highlighting the inherent instability of codependency.

Melody Beattie describes codependence as a behavioral condition where one person enables another person's addiction, poor mental health, immaturity, irresponsibility, or under-achievement (2022). I hold the view that we all engage in codependent dynamics to differing degrees since we all have underdeveloped inner parts or psychological blind spots (shadow parts) that we project onto our partners.

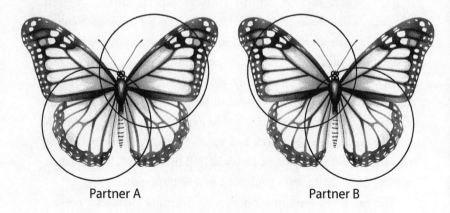

Partner A   Partner B

In a codependent dynamic, each partner relies excessively on aspects of their partner's personality in order to function as depicted by the diagonal Venn diagrams above.

People often express feeling like a parent in relationships or being treated like a child. Sometimes, the partner in the parent role is more dominant and, interestingly, sometimes the partner in the role of the child rules the roost! The latter is the case with Tony and Cheryl.

Tony, with a huff of frustration, snaps, "Cheryl, where did you put my work papers?! I can't find them anywhere, and I need them now!

Cheryl responds in a calming tone, "I put them on your bedside table. I thought you'd see them there. Let me go get them for you."

Tony, whining slightly, says, "Why can't you just leave my things where they are? You always move my stuff and I can never find it!"

"I was just trying to be helpful. I'll make sure to ask next time," Cheryl soothingly responds (silently resenting the mess Tony often leaves in the shared household areas).

This dialogue highlights Tony's excessive reliance on Cheryl to keep track of his belongings and his reactive, childlike frustration when things aren't as he expects them to be. It also reveals his sense of entitlement to cause disarray in communal areas of the house.

Cheryl, on the other hand, takes on a parental role, caring for Tony even when faced with his complaints and criticism. She keeps her need for tidiness to herself. Tony is dominant and Cheryl is submissive in this example, despite the fact that she takes on the role of parent and he acts like a child.

Initially, this parent-child dynamic can work in a complementary way for both parties. Tony, the "child" finds comfort in Cheryl's reliable, nurturing nature. Cheryl, the "parent," derives satisfaction from being needed as a caretaker and feels a sense of control. She experiences a sense of purpose and competence in smoothing out their daily challenges. This structure provides them both with a safety net, shielding them from having to face certain responsibilities or confront their less developed shadow parts.

As time goes on, problems will develop when one or both partners grow and change, no longer happy in the prescribed roles. Cheryl might start feeling overwhelmed or taken for granted, and resent the imbalance of emotional labor in the relationship. She may yearn for a partner who meets her as an equal, sharing responsibilities, emotional burdens, and decision making. Meanwhile, Tony may grapple with feelings of inadequacy, frustration, and dependency, as he constantly leans on Cheryl for guidance and support. He might start to feel stifled, longing for autonomy and resenting the unspoken implication that he can't manage his own affairs. The symbiosis between them begins to fade. Their dynamic, once comforting, may begin to sow seeds of discontent, leading both partners to question the sustainability and health of their bond.

* * *

I experienced codependence firsthand as a young woman. One evening, in my early twenties, my old high school friend Barb and I were dancing the night away at Don Cherry's in Hamilton. I loved dancing. It was a way to express myself—and maybe even get some attention. Although we may have looked drunk, neither of us had a drop of alcohol as we twirled around, covering most of the dance floor, song after song.

Don Cherry's had a bunch of billiard tables too. I had grown up with a pool table at home, so I was a bit of a shark. Barb and I were busy knocking them in when I noticed his eyes on me. It wasn't long before I was playing a game with this flirtatious guy named Jeff, happy to show off my moves.

Barb and I frequented that bar, playing pool and dancing Thursday after Thursday, since that was "lady's night." I'd look for Jeff as I entered and find him there, or see him when he entered. Things became friendlier between us week after week, until we became an item.

But it wasn't long before an unhealthy dynamic emerged between us. He was dominant and I was submissive. He was aggressive and I was more passive. He was street-smart and I was naïve. He led and I followed. It was fun at first. I needed someone like him since I didn't have much of a sense of self, nor much of an agenda besides not feeling alone.

I didn't know my own likes or dislikes, but Jeff thought of fun places to go and fun things to do. He made the best BBQed chicken and mashed potatoes ever. He was attentive and that was enough for me at the time. There were moments of disagreement, but Jeff's charm kept things going. We seemed to complement one another initially.

Soon enough, the red flags became flashing neon signs. Jeff would get jealous if I looked at a waiter in a restaurant. He started calling me derogatory names. He had things to say about where I went, my family, and who my friends were. While I had initially enjoyed and even needed his constant availability and attention, things came to a head when he hitchhiked almost 400 kilometers in the pouring rain to Algonquin Park, where I'd gone camping with Barb, just to keep tabs on me.

I had been quite easy to control initially. Jeff blamed me for our problems, and I thought he must be right since I was inexperienced in so many ways, including with men. I spent my time feeling guilty and crying, while he was filled with righteous indignation for my most recent "crime."

When I finally started standing up for myself, all hell broke loose. I called Jeff an "asshole" and he looked completely shocked as he blurted out, "You can't speak to me that way!" We were trapped in the duality of dominance and submission, and me trying to fight for more dignity as I got to know myself better was not working. It just escalated the conflict. In the end, it seemed as though I only had two options: to submit or leave him. I left.

* * *

Relationships need stability, and hierarchy can appear to achieve that, at least in the world of branches, on the surface. As long as both partners are relatively content in their positions, they have stability but at the expense of equality. Maintaining stability while achieving equality is a challenge. Thankfully, we have three powerful practices to assist us in doing so. They are to *appreciate, collaborate*, and *compensate*.

The first practice is to *appreciate* your partner. Envision a sunflower turning its bright face to bask in the sun's golden rays, soaking in the warm sense of appreciation the light gives. This radiant example demonstrates the power of recognizing and valuing your partner. You are like those warm rays of sunshine when you appreciate your partner. Appreciation breathes life into relationships. It invigorates, inspires, and builds confidence no matter how big or small the appreciated act may be. By appreciating your partner, you not only recognize how your partner pleases you, you also amplify positivity within yourself.

Now, I know what you might be thinking, *Oh, I do appreciate my partner, I feel it inside.* That's wonderful, and it's a great start, but appreciation isn't just an emotion tucked away inside your chest; it's an action, a demonstration—it's something you need to express overtly, showing it so your partner can perceive it through their five senses. Showing appreciation requires that you take that warm feeling and put it out there for your partner to see, hear, and feel.

We're all guilty of taking each other for granted at times. It's easy to fall into the trap of thinking, *Well, my partner should be doing those things; it's part of being an adult. Do I really need to give a round of applause or blow a trumpet every time they do their share?* The answer is, "Yes!" It's about acknowledging efforts, big or small, that contribute to the shared life you're building. It sends a powerful message: *I see you; I value you, and I acknowledge your contribution.* A simple thank-you goes a long way and it's so easy to do. Studies show we tend to repeat feedback. Why not just do it?

Dr. John Gottman and Joan DeClaire suggest fostering a "culture of appreciation" in relationships (2002). They believe partners should habitually look for things to appreciate in one another—rather than constantly pointing out flaws or issues. By focusing on and voicing appreciation, couples build a buffer of positivity that protects their connection. They found that couples who maintain a culture of appreciation tend to be more resilient during hard times and feel more positively about each other and their marriage overall.

Expressing appreciation when your partner works overtime to earn more money for the household might make the exertion seem worth it to your partner, despite feeling stretched and tired. Saying thank you to your partner for being a good parent and driving the kids to yet another sport event, adds value and a sense that you're in it together, working for the same goal even though you play different roles.

Twice a day, take a moment to notice something you appreciate about your partner's qualities or contributions. It could be something they've done, such as taking care of a chore or task, or a trait they possess, like their sense of humor, kindness, or resilience. Be as specific as possible. Once you've noticed something, articulate your appreciation and the positive impact it has on you. Compliment your partner's contribution. Do it in front of others, if possible. Use words to express what you noticed and how it made you feel. A simple formula might be, "I noticed you (insert positive behavior). I (insert positive thought or feeling). Thank you." For instance, "I noticed you took out the trash this morning. I think we make a good team. Thank you." Or, "I noticed your patience with the kids today. I felt joyful. Thank you."

But don't stop at words. Enhance your verbal appreciation with nonverbal cues. Your body language, facial expression, posture, tone of voice, and eye contact can all amplify the sincerity of your appreciation. As you express it, let your face light up with a smile. Turn your body toward your partner, showing them how pleased you are, even without words. Keep your voice calm, soft, and sincere to convey your genuine feeling. Make eye contact and hold it for a moment, creating a deeper connection with your partner. And don't forget to add a warm gesture, like a touch on the shoulder, a gentle hug, or a moment of holding your partner's hand. These subtle gestures often speak much louder than words, reinforcing the depth of your sentiment.

The second key practice to attain the principle of equality in your interdependent relationship is to *collaborate*. We've all heard the saying, "It takes two to tango!" Indeed, imagine a dance where you and your partner move harmoniously, complementing each other's movements. Each of you brings your own dance moves, yet together, you create a fluid and mesmerizing flow between you. The tango definitely requires collaboration, and so does a shared partnership.

Collaboration plays a vital role in fostering a sense of equality and interdependence between partners in a relationship. When couples collaborate, they engage in a process of sharing responsibilities, decision-making, and problem-solving, which reinforces the idea that both parties are equally important and valued in the relationship.

Collaboration involves active communication and negotiation, allowing each partner to voice their opinions, needs, and concerns. This open dialogue ensures that both individuals are heard and understood, creating a platform for mutual respect. When partners feel that their viewpoints are equally considered, it enhances their sense of being valued and respected in the relationship.

Collaborative problem-solving encourages empathy and understanding. By working together to overcome challenges, partners get to know each other's strengths, weaknesses, and comfort levels, which fosters deeper emotional connection. By working together and valuing each other's perspectives, the couple also ensures that no single partner is unfairly burdened or disadvantaged.

The ability to collaborate is a universally valuable tool, applicable to any challenge a couple might face. Collaboration involves the following five steps:

1. **Open discussion:** Identify and voice the issue or challenge together.

2. **Joint brainstorming:** Share ideas and solutions openly, valuing each person's perspective.

3. **Agreeing on strategies:** Find common ground and decide on actionable steps.

4. **Implementing together:** Put your plan into action, sharing the responsibilities.

5. **Regular check-ins:** Revisit the issue periodically to assess and adjust as needed.

Using these steps, you can jointly tackle any hurdle, be it financial planning, deciding on parenting strategies, determining who does what around the house, or even choosing where to spend your holidays.

Pick an issue—maybe not the hottest-button issue, but one that you can tackle with success. Get started on the five steps of collaboration. By moving outside your comfort zones in these domains, you ensure both partners feel valued and heard, and are actively involved in making decisions. Each and every time you collaborate, whether it's on weekend plans or home renovation ideas, you relegate the duality of dominance and submission to the sidelines and inch closer to equality and effective interdependence.

A third key practice in attaining equality in your couple relationship is to *compensate*. In case you've already gone there, I'm *not* suggesting you pay your partner to do chores. Rather, visualize a seesaw with you and your partner sitting on either end. For the seesaw to maintain a balanced and enjoyable rhythm, both of you need to make an effort. If one of you pushes too hard or doesn't push enough, the balance is lost.

Compensation in a relationship is about recognizing when your partner might be facing extra challenges or carrying a heavier load, resulting in a lack of equality between you. You compensate your partner for the inequality you perceive by adjusting your contributions accordingly. It's a balancing act, where partners give, pull back, or make up for something that created a sense of inequality in order to proactively maintain harmony and mutual satisfaction.

It's not about *getting* compensation. *It's about giving it.* It's not a moment-to-moment, tit-for-tat scorekeeping approach, but involves zooming out and considering the big picture by asking yourself, "Am I benefitting at my partner's expense in our relationship?" and "If so, how can I make efforts to balance the scale proactively?"

Originally developed by psychologist John Stacey Adams in 1963, equity theory posits that individuals are motivated by a desire to be treated fairly in their work relationships, equating fairness with balance between what they put in and what they get out. In

1978, Walster, Walster, and Berscheid extended the equity theory to include its application in intimate relationships. They found that if one partner feels they are putting more into the relationship than they are getting out, they may feel distress, dissatisfaction, or resentment. On the other hand, if a partner feels they are receiving more than they deserve or contribute, they may feel guilt or shame. All of these negative emotions get in the way of connection and healthy interdependence.

For example, it is not uncommon for one partner's career to take precedence over the others. When children are sick, the responsibility to stay home from work may invariably fall on the other partner, who might also assume a larger share of household chores. The whole family may even be required to move to a new city to support the partner's career. While these types of sacrifices are often made willingly out of love and commitment, they can lead to resentment over time if they are not acknowledged and proactively compensated for by the partner whose career is favored.

Similarly, one partner may earn more and subsequently have more say in how money is spent. Without conscious efforts to rebalance the scales through compensation, such patterns can significantly strain the bond between partners.

One partner may end up shouldering the "mental load"—the daily demands of organizing family life, including any array of things such as scheduling doctor's appointments, or making sure there's cat litter. These contributions are often overlooked and can lead to profound imbalances in a relationship.

By actively recognizing and discussing daily dynamics, couples can cultivate an awareness of where compensation might be needed, fostering a more balanced, equitable, and interdependent relationship.

First, think about potential inequalities in your relationship, where you come out "ahead" and your partner gets the short end of the stick. This requires some brutal honesty and the willingness to admit the ways you may be benefitting and enjoying life at your partner's expense.

Second, mention your observations to your partner and open up a conversation to see if they perceive it the same way and if they are carrying any related resentment. Try to talk about it using the principle of surrender from Chapter Five, and its related practices of being defenseless, present, and open.

Third, together, brainstorm ways you could even out the scales by making conscious efforts to compensate your partner. The goal is to show your partner you see them, value them, and are willing to take action and exert effort to reduce or counteract perceived inequalities. The ideas generated between the two partners need to resonate as relevant, meaningful, and valuable to the partner being compensated.

For example, if one partner's career has been favored, that partner might take care of dinner and the kids one evening a week while the other partner engages in a hobby or course. Or if one partner manages the mental load of running the household, the other partner could take it upon themselves to plan quality couple time twice a month.

The last step is to take responsibility for executing the agreement or plan, for implementing the compensatory activity. This is not the same as acting out of guilt. The aim is to honor your connection proactively and avoid future blowups due to accumulated hurts and resentments. Take compensation seriously. Make it a priority. It's not a payback but a "pay it forward" kind of attitude to prevent your partner from feeling taken advantage of or taken for granted, and to keep things balanced in the long run. It's good to be on the receiving end of benefits in your relationship so make sure your partner experiences their fair share of good things too!

* * *

Emma makes more money than her husband David. Let's hear how they collaborate to build the principle of equality in their relationship:

Emma: "David, we need to talk about our finances. I've noticed you've been withdrawing more from our joint account lately."

David: "Yeah, I know, some extra expenses came up this month."

Emma: "It seems these extra expenses are becoming more frequent. What are you buying?"

David: "Well, I know you earn more, but we have plenty of money. I didn't think it would be a big deal."

Emma: "That's not the point. It's not about who earns more. Our money is shared. But we should be discussing these things."

David: "But that's just it. It feels like because you earn more, you have more say in our finances. It's like my input matters less when we get into these arguments. You always get the last word."

Emma: "It's not about having more say. It's about making decisions together, discussing and planning, not acting unilaterally."

David: "But can you see how that makes me feel, like I'm not an equal partner because I earn less? It's like you're the dominant one here, and I'm like a child, having to ask for an allowance or get your permission to buy some candy at the corner store."

Emma: "That's not how I want you to feel, but I don't know what to do."

David: "I don't know. Maybe if I had some discretionary money, I wouldn't feel this way. I work too ya know."

Emma: "Okay, what if we set aside some money for each of us every month, that we can spend, no questions asked? That way, we both have some freedom without straining the budget."

David: That a good idea. It gives us both a bit of independence without having to hide what we buy or feel guilty."

Emma: "Exactly. It's not about control. It's about equality. Let's figure out an approximate amount that makes sense for both of us."

The Appreciation Jar Exercise

Materials:
- A jar (or any container)
- Small pieces of paper or note cards
- Pens

Instructions:

1. Label your jar the "Appreciation Jar."

2. Each day, as partners, write down something you appreciate about the other person on a piece of paper. It can be an act of kindness, a trait you admire, or something your partner did that day that made you smile or feel loved.

3. Fold the note and place it in the jar.

4. Make it a point to share your appreciation notes at a dedicated time each week—perhaps Friday evening or Sunday morning. Take turns reading the notes out loud.

5. As you read the notes, make sure to make eye contact and thank your partner sincerely.

Over time, this simple exercise can cultivate a culture of appreciation in your relationship. It not only helps you notice and value each other's contributions more but also builds a reservoir of positive feelings and memories that can reinforce the principle of equality in your relationship.

7

Generosity

"Real giving is when we give to our spouses what's important to
them, whether we understand it, like it, agree with it, or not."
– Michele Weiner-Davis

*O*nce upon a time, in the vibrant, high-paced city of
Chicago, a young and ambitious couple found themselves
working at the same prestigious law firm. M and B were
both driven individuals, yet they discovered an incredible connection that extended beyond their shared passion for justice. Their
ice-cream dates and long city walks were testaments to their mutual
generosity—the giving of time and attention to one another despite
the pressures of their hectic schedules.

The strength of their bond was tested when B revealed his aspirations
to run for public office. It was a decision that would propel the couple
into uncharted territory of countless sacrifices and intense scrutiny. The
peaceful simplicity of their life was to be disrupted by a whirlwind of
campaign trails, speeches, and relentless media attention.

But this is no fairy tale romance. It's a real story about a real
couple, and you certainly know who they are—Michelle and Barack
Obama. As a Canadian, I don't have any particular affiliation with

American politics. But celebrities, whether they're politicians or movie stars, often live their lives in the public eye and can be good examples of the principles of interdependent relationships at play. The love story between Barack and Michelle has lessons for all of us.

When the Obamas moved into the White House, their seven-year-old daughter, Sasha, was the youngest to live there since John F. Kennedy, Jr. Her sister, Malia, was only ten. Through most of their young lives, their parents had faced the challenges of raising them in the midst of rough-and-tumble American politics. They survived as a couple and a family through the spirit of generosity that was a cornerstone of Michelle and Barack's relationship.

Uncertainty didn't stop Michelle from supporting Barack's dream. She chose to put any concerns she may have had aside, demonstrating an extraordinary level of generosity. Her spirit not only gave Barack the strength to face the fierce political landscape but grounded him during the rigors of the campaign trail. Barack acknowledged the sacrifices Michelle was making. He admired her resilience and her commitment to supporting his dreams while still managing their home and raising their two daughters.

The Obamas navigated their way through the tumultuous waters of Barack's political ambitions, guided by a spirit of generosity. A willingness to give time, attention, and emotional support to each other strengthened their bond during these challenging years. It was their acts of giving—not just of material things but of patience, understanding, and mutual support—that helped them overcome obstacles and maintain a connection.

* * *

Generosity is like a river that flows freely, nourishing everything it touches, enriching the land without expecting an immediate pay back. The third principle of the Butterfly Blueprint—*generosity*—holds a pivotal place in cultivating a healthy interdependent partnership. It embodies the act of *freely* giving of oneself—of one's time, patience, understanding, and emotional availability—for the benefit of the relationship. As Mahatma Gandhi wisely stated, "Generosity consists not in the sum given, but the manner in which it is bestowed." Similarly, Mother Teresa emphasized, "It is not how much we give but how much love we put into the giving." This principle, when incorporated, deepens connection and strengthens mutual respect.

Just as each set of wings must delicately support the body of a butterfly—the core of their union—for it to flutter gracefully, partners in a relationship must generously contribute to the well-being of their shared connection. When partners are generous toward each other, they willingly invest in the relationship, contributing to the shared emotional bank account and inspiring each other to follow suit. When faced with challenges or disagreements, the reservoir of mutual generosity—like money in the bank—provides a buffer of understanding and patience.

Generosity manifests as kindness, thoughtfulness, and the willingness to share time, effort, and resources. On one end, being generous involves actively contributing to the well-being and happiness of your partner by offering support during challenging times, surprising them with gestures of love, or simply being attentive to their needs. On the other end, it's just as important to being open to accepting what your partner offers. This includes being graciously receptive to your partner's gestures, efforts, and support. Showing you value what your partner brings to the relationship encourages a reciprocal flow of affection and care. Ultimately, this mutual exchange of kindness and respect fosters a deep connection and a strong foundation of sharing in the relationship. It's about understanding that both partners have a role to play in attaining the principle of generosity.

The principle of generosity in a couple's relationship, while transformative, contains a subtle duality dilemma: the delicate balance between *giving and receiving*. This reminds me of Joey's funny speech at Monica and Chandler's wedding on the sitcom *Friends*. While Joey hit the nail on the head when it comes to "a love based on giving and receiving as well as having and sharing," it's not as easy or funny as he made it sound.

Ideally, giving and receiving should seamlessly integrate, fostering mutual fulfillment, which is nicely demonstrated in the following story about the guest and the host. The host thoughtfully prepares a meal—a gift of time and effort—which the guest graciously receives and enjoys. In turn, the host receives pleasure from seeing the guest's enjoyment of the meal, and thus, both benefit and love comes full circle. However, giving and receiving love more often turns into a transactional, scorekeeping comparison or contest, hindering the flow of generosity and becoming a source of friction.

This happens when partners start keeping tabs on who's done what for whom and for how long, turning the relationship into a ledger of debits and credits. The spirit of generosity is clouded by the quest for fairness. While reciprocation and mutuality are important when it comes to giving and receiving, fairness becomes a problem when it turns into meticulous bookkeeping.

This mindset can breed resentment and a feeling of constant indebtedness, blocking the flow of shared abundance and mutual fulfillment. No one likes to feel like they owe someone something, so receiving is sometimes avoided for this reason. As the ledger of debits and credits grows, it can spawn sneaky behavior in the relationship—the act of giving with strings attached. Partners may give not out of wholehearted generosity, but as a calculated move to secure something for themselves in return, to obligate the other to reciprocate. These are not free gifts but investments with the covert—if sometimes unconscious—expectation of getting what one wants *for oneself*.

* * *

I threw a fiftieth birthday party for Matthew a few years ago, in our home. I catered his favorite Indian food and invited his local South African friends. I organized our daughter to come and take him out on some random excursion while the guests sneakily filed in and found a place to hide. When Matthew finally came home and entered the room where the party was waiting for him, he was indeed, "SURPRISE-D!!!"

After eating and enjoying an ice-cream cake, he sat in the spotlight while we shared our stories about him. It was a huge success. He loved it. On top of all that, I took us on a cruise in the Caribbean as a birthday gift. Neither of us had ever been on a cruise before, so it was quite a magical experience having breakfast on our balcony as the sun rose over the endless ocean horizon.

Just over a year later, it was my fiftieth, and of course, I was hoping for the efforts to be reciprocated. So much for my "generosity." I had given with strings or expectations attached! I wanted Matthew to do the same for me, or something similar and special.

My birthday occurred one year into the COVID-19 era, when everything was shut down. We didn't have many options—at least outside of the house. It fell relatively flat. Matthew always remembers my birthday. He bought dinner and gifts; however, I was disappointed. I wanted him to make more of a fuss.

I told myself stories about Matthew not caring and thought up lots of in-house birthday celebration options he could have planned for the two of us, but in the end, I realized that my expectations didn't align with his way of expressing love and care. It comes up from time to time in a scorekeeping kind of way, when I get caught up in the duality dilemma of giving and receiving in our relationship. This type of mindset blocks the flow of generosity between us at times.

* * *

While gestures may appear to be altruistic on the surface in the world of branches, ulterior motives such as seeking admiration often lurk beneath in the roots. When we engage in generosity, we may be striving for a sense of superiority or virtue. We may want to side-step conflicts or even use giving as a means of control. We might be trying to earn forgiveness, get sex, or reinforce dependency.

Similarly, receiving can feel more like taking, becoming an act of coercion, trying to bend your partner into doing what you want. Taking might include demanding apologies, seeking affirmations of love, nagging to get things done, or pushing for sex. The undercurrent of control, entitlement, and expectation taints the spirit of generosity, turning it into a tool of manipulation and breeding discontent.

Human beings are instinctively attuned to sense when a gift comes with strings attached or serves the giver more than the receiver. Mirror neurons help us detect "strings." In his book *Mirroring People* (2008), neuroscientist Marco Iacoboni posits that mirror neurons, which are brain cells that activate both when we perform an action and when we see someone else perform the same action, allow us to discern the other person's intention when performing the act, whether they are aiming for self-benefit or the benefit of the other. An obvious example of this comes from an episode of *The Simpsons* where Homer gives Marge a bowling ball for her birthday.

As it turns out, many of us seldom experience true, unadulterated generosity. At its core, generosity is about *freely* giving on behalf of the relationship and graciously receiving while keeping the connection in mind and heart.

* * *

It was January 26, 1996, and my son was two and a half. It was a cold and blustery Saturday morning. We were in the dead of a Canadian winter as I made my way from Brantford, in my trusty Honda Civic, to a Women's Center meeting in Hamilton. I was on the board of directors. My son's empty car seat and his toys were in the back of the car, and I was driving alone when blizzard conditions set in....

"LaRose...LaRooooose!!!" My first words in the emergency room, a few days after the accident, before I had even opened my eyes, were my babysitter's last name, "LaRose." My first thought was for my son.

As I became conscious, my mother told me I had been hit by an 18-wheeler transport truck, which had been traveling in the opposite direction on the highway. It had lost control in the blizzard, jack-knifed, crossed the median, and demolished my car, which had also caught fire. Luckily, a man who was driving behind me had a fire-extinguisher with him and put out the flames before first responders arrived on the scene.

I had my twenty-fifth birthday in the hospital that year and was amazed at how my room filled with balloons, gifts, and cards carrying loving messages, some from old high school friends I'd lost touch with. It was one of the best birthdays ever, as I laid happily, immobile in my hospital bed, my right leg and ankle crushed, my teeth knocked out— with a head injury, other puncture wounds, a broken thumb—black and blue from head to toe. The hospital social worker had told my parents my chances of survival weren't good. I was lucky to be alive.

You might wonder why "I laid happily" in my hospital bed while crushed to pieces. As you might have guessed, I didn't experience a lot of generosity in the form of attention while growing up. In fact, I had fantasized as a child about how good it must feel to go to the hospital and get all that attention from the staff.

I grew up in the country, in the middle of nowhere. Both of my parents worked fulltime and commuted to work. My dad was gone before we woke up and wouldn't get home until after 6:00 p.m., at which time he had marking to do since he was a teacher. My mom worked the afternoon shift for years. Like so many families, mine also has a history of mental health issues, including severe depression and anxiety.

I don't blame my parents, who had their own traumas; they did their best just as I did the best I could as a single mom for my son. Everyone has parents who have histories and stories of their own. Suffering is an inherent and inevitable part of our complex human lives, and *it's nobody's fault!*

Nature made life this way, with the good and the bad, the pleasure and the pain, the joys and the sorrows, the two sides of so many coins. I appreciate everything I have so much more because of the contrast between where I've been and where I am now.

So, I "laid happily" in my hospital bed because I experienced a lot of generosity in the aftermath of my encounter with the 18-wheeler. The life-saving actions of the man who stepped into the chaotic event and risked his safety to put out the fire enveloping my car was testament to the purest form of generosity. He may have very well *saved my life*—with no expectation of reciprocation or gain, no transactional underpinnings or manipulative strings attached. It was utterly selfless and purely heroic. He could have been harmed, but he helped me anyways.

The same can be said of the outpouring of thoughtful gifts and cards on my birthday. These gestures held no ledger keeping score, no enumeration of debts to be repaid. I was incapacitated, bound to my hospital bed. I couldn't pay them back. Yet the warmth and generosity I received felt boundless. The only act of generosity I could return was simply telling the driver of the transport truck to go on with his life when he called me in the hospital, crying, to express how sorry he was.

* * *

The first key practice of generosity is to *nurture the connection between you.* Love is like a pet you have to feed every day. Your relationship is a living entity, a creature that needs to be lovingly attended to every day, without fail—like a cat that needs fed, a dog that needs walked, or a delicate plant that craves sunlight, water, and fertilizer. You don't make excuses not to feed your fur-babies. You aren't stubborn when it comes to caring for your children each day! You know these things have to be done, or you will lose who and what you love most in life.

You might not think of nurturing a pet or a plant as being generous, but it is. You are helping another life form *live* through your efforts. You are adding loving effort and conscious intention. It's easy to forget relationships are also living things that continually evolve and will wither and die without proper attention and TLC (tender loving care).

I often hear couples sigh in exasperation: "A relationship shouldn't be this hard." But let's face it: relationships are work and require daily effort, especially when your partner faces extraordinary stressors—whether due to work, personal loss, health challenges, or even when they might be "hangry" or PMS'ing (hopefully not both at the same time!).

* * *

Matthew and I love our pet dog, Charlie. He's a Jack Russell, or Jack *Rascal*, as I like to fondly call him since he has a mind of his own! Charlie is definitely the life of the party, and we can all learn a lot about generosity from our dogs. Like most dogs, he runs to the door, tail wagging, tongue licking, and puppy-dog eyes locked on Matthew when he comes home after work.

One day, I decided to try to "top the dog" and ran alongside Charlie, competing for who could be the most adoring of Matthew, pretending to wag my "tail" and lick Matthew's face. He grinned from ear to ear and it became a kind of daily ritual for a while. It was my effort to "feed the pet" of our relationship, somewhat literally!

* * *

Some of the most significant and sincere gifts you can offer your partner are your time, attention, and affection. Tokens of love and respect need not be grand gestures, nor do they have to cost a lot. Instead, small, genuine acts that transmit warmth and care add "money in the emotional bank account." A warm hug, eye contact, a helping hand, a thoughtful note left on the counter, or a simple compliment can all hit the mark. Even just saying, "I'm glad you're here" is nice for anyone to hear.

Echoing this sentiment, the lyrics from Jeffrey Osborne's 1982 hit song "On the Wings of Love" resonate profoundly: "Just smile for me and let the day begin / You are the sunshine that lights my heart within." These lines capture the essence of offering simple acts of love and care, illuminating how small gestures can deeply touch the heart and strengthen the bonds of love.

In his book *Atomic Habits* (2018), James Clear emphasizes the transformational power of small, daily changes in creating significant long-term results. The main thing is to be consistent. Just like doing the dishes and the laundry, expressions of love need to be daily, no matter how you feel and what else is going on—no excuses. Get the ball of generosity rolling in your relationship and start with something small. Build on that each day, or week, so you're regularly "feeding the pet." Part of this consistency is detaching from the immediate outcome; it's about the act of generosity itself, not just the response you receive (or don't receive).

An essential tool in nurturing your relationship daily is understanding and implementing *The Five Love Languages* (2010). This concept and book, developed by Dr. Gary Chapman, posits that people have different ways they prefer to receive love: words of affirmation, acts of service, receiving gifts, quality time, and physical touch. Each person has a primary love language that satisfies their emotional needs more than the others.

For instance, one might feel loved when they hear verbal compliments, while another prefers spending quality time together. Understanding your partner's love language is like learning their dietary preferences, allowing you to provide the "food" that best nourishes and pleases your partner and, subsequently, your relationship or butterfly. Regularly doing this will ensure the bond remains robust and vibrant.

The second key practice to invite more generosity into your relationship is to *say what you do want*. Assertively expressing what you *do* want gives your partner a chance of succeeding at being generous; you empower your partner to come through for you; you teach them and show them how to please you. Most people are well aware of what they *don't* want or *don't* like and easily communicate dissatisfaction to their partners through complaints and criticism. Sometimes this is referred to as giving "constructive criticism" so the partner can learn to do things better next time.

However, research suggests that there may be no such thing as *constructive* criticism in love relationships. Eisenberger, Lieberman, and Williams's research found that areas of the brain that light up during physical pain are also activated when we experience social pain, like the sting of criticism from a loved one (2003). This means that when you critique your partner, it can literally feel like a punch to their brain. Criticism is also identified as one of the four horsemen of the apocalypse in *Ten Lessons to Transform Your Marriage* (Gottman et al., 2006, pg. 5), which outlines detrimental communication patterns that predict relationship challenges and eventual dissolution. The other three "horsemen" are defensiveness, contempt, and stonewalling.

Frequently in counseling, the same partners who criticize and complain say, "I don't know" when asked directly what they need or what they *do* want. Sometimes, they have never been asked that question before, so it's new to consider the answer. Nevertheless, understanding your own wants and desires is necessary in order to give your partner a fighting chance to fulfill them. Generosity requires cooperation from both partners to hit the bullseye.

Otherwise, your partner has to read your mind or play guessing games trying to figure out how to make you happy, which many find frustrating. So many partners try hard but are met with disappointment and a sense of failure. "He got me flowers, but I'm allergic," Sonya shared. "He packed the car, but I needed help with the kids," Elizabeth moaned. "She cleaned the house, but I wanted her to sit and talk to me," Mateo expressed.

This is why getting to know yourself or your own set of wings is so important in building a healthy, strong, interdependent relationship. Without desire, longing, or a "vessel" for the filling, there's no place to put generosity, just like there's no place for food without hunger.

The movie *Runaway Bride*, starring Julia Roberts and Richard Gere, nicely illustrates this concept. Julia Roberts plays the role of Maggie Carpenter, a woman notorious for leaving her fiancés standing at the altar. The film features several of Maggie's ex-fiancés, including Brian, Bob, and Gill, who all experienced her indecisiveness firsthand. Throughout the movie, Maggie unconsciously adopts her fiancé's preferred way of cooking eggs, highlighting her lack of self-awareness and personal preferences.

Richard Gere, playing the character of Ike Graham, a reporter covering Maggie's numerous runaway incidents, notices this pattern and challenges Maggie to figure out her own egg preference. He prompts her to explore her desires without the influence of a romantic partner.

After several humorous and heartfelt trials, in the end, Maggie discovers how *she* likes her eggs cooked: eggs benedict (good choice!). This revelation about her own preference becomes a crucial step toward fostering healthier interdependent relationships. Echoing the words of Yung Pueblo in his book *Inward* (2018, p. 32), "if you are far away from yourself, how could you ever be close to another?"

After doing the work to get to *know thyself*, it's also essential to *show thyself*, by letting your partner in on your new insights. The honest—even assertive—revelation of your wants and needs allows your partner to understand and fulfill your desires better. Sharing your desires openly isn't the same as demanding, expecting, forcing, or coercing. It simply means putting them on the table or showing your hand so your partner can get to know them too.

A common stumbling block in relationships is the belief that your partner should inherently know your desires without being told. Many feel they shouldn't have to articulate their needs or wants, thinking, *If my partner truly loved me, he or she would just know what I need and saying it cheapens it.* Of course, it's also nice when your partner makes the effort to pay attention to you and learns your likes and dislikes by listening and making observations. But expecting your partner to figure out what you enjoy when you come across like a closed book who doesn't need anything is a little unfair. This mindset impedes the flow of generosity and understanding. I've witnessed many partners say, "This is the first time I'm hearing this," in couples counseling sessions when their significant other expresses a desire in a calm way. The partner often expresses how pleased and relieved they are to be told directly and to be "let in" in this way.

Many people resist showing and expressing their desires and say, "If I say it, my partner will just do it! Not because they want to, but just because I said it!" But isn't this a positive response? When your partner acts on your wishes solely to please you, without any direct benefit to themselves, when they might even rather *not* do it, it demonstrates their commitment to caring for both you and the bond you share. This isn't about coercion or unreasonable demands. Articulating your desires is distinctly different from expecting your partner to automatically fulfill them, without question. It's about open communication and mutual understanding, not obligation or duty.

Getting to know yourself emotionally is key to knowing what you need and want. Each emotion is accompanied by a distinct action tendency or impulse to behave in a certain way. Anger prompts confrontation and assertiveness. Fear leads one to self-protect or avoid. Joy encourages one to engage or embrace. Understanding and feeling your emotions will help you to be able to say what you *do* want to do or receive, enabling your partner to be generous with you.

Mindfulness meditation is one way to turn inward and get to know yourself. It's all about staying present and paying close attention to your thoughts, feelings, and bodily sensations without judgment. By sitting quietly and focusing on your breath, you witness your internal landscape, revealing desires and needs that might be buried beneath the surface of conscious awareness.

I used the yoga and body scan meditation CDs of Dr. Jon Kabat-Zinn for years after my car accident. They helped me heal from severe chronic back pain. This type of meditation guides you to concentrate on different parts of your body, bringing awareness to any physical sensations. Often, these sensations can reflect emotional states and tension (1990). By checking in with the body in this way, you can gain a better understanding of your internal world of roots.

For those who feel anxious when meditating, there are other means of self-exploration. Journaling offers a gateway to self-discovery, allowing you to chronicle and process your emotions, eventually revealing patterns that illuminate your likes and dislikes. Similarly, an artistic endeavor—be it painting, dancing, or playing an instrument—can provide a unique medium to get in touch with feelings that words might not capture. Embracing solitude—whether it's a reflective nature walk or a solo trip—creates opportunity for introspection. Finally, spending time with children and observing their free and spontaneous self-expression can help you reconnect to your inner child's desires, the life force inside you.

The third key practice in invoking the principle of generosity in relationships is to *express an attitude of gratitude*. Gratitude is much like sunlight—a transformative force that melts away negativity, highlighting the beauty and warmth in everyday moments.

Gratitude shifts our focus from what's lacking or problematic to what's abundant and *right* in our lives and partnerships. Life is full of dualities: the pluses and the minuses, and the half-full or half-empty glasses. Research consistently indicates that expressing gratitude within a relationship can greatly enhance its quality and longevity. It shifts the focus from negative behaviors to positive ones, fostering a more supportive and loving environment. Positive reinforcement strengthens bonds and reduces conflict in love relationships.

While appreciation (a practice from Chapter Six) and gratitude are both positive responses, appreciation is more about acknowledging the value or significance of something or someone. It's an active recognition of your partner's worth or inherent goodness. You can appreciate your partner from a distance. Gratitude, on the other hand, is the emotion felt when we realize we've received a tangible benefit. It's a feeling of thankfulness for the blessings you didn't necessarily earn or expect.

Expressing gratitude begins by paying close attention to the ways your partner enriches your life. As you cultivate this awareness, you'll find plenty of moments—big and small—you can be grateful for: the way your partner prepares your tea or coffee in the morning, just the way you like it; or how your partner listens to you after a long day. Maybe your partner's touch warms your heart just when you need it most. Don't let these moments slip by without expressing gratitude!

You can express gratitude verbally by regularly telling your partner how their actions impact your life in a positive way. It's essential to be specific and genuine with your words. Instead of just saying, "You're a great partner," you might say, "I'm grateful for your patience with me yesterday afternoon when I was stressed. It truly made a difference." Gratitude can also be incorporated into your daily rituals as a couple. This might involve expressing something you're grateful for regularly during dinner or before bedtime during pillow talk.

In addition to saying it with words, you can show gratitude through actions and gestures. This might involve preparing a special meal, offering a hug, or assisting with everyday chores while also expressing what you're grateful for. Finally, consider writing letters of gratitude to your partner. Whether on special occasions or just as a surprise, a heartfelt note can be a powerful way to express your feelings of gratitude. Cultivating gratitude in your relationship is a practice that requires consistency and intention. The more you practice, the more natural it will feel since habit becomes a second nature.

* * *

After a stressful day at work, Liam found himself stopping by the grocery store on his way home. He decided to prepare dinner for Sophie, something simple but requiring a bit of effort—a home-made lasagna.

Back at their apartment, Liam was taking the lasagna out of the oven when Sophie walked in. She had spent the day in back-to-back meetings at her insurance job and was still full from a late lunch. She wasn't thinking of dinner until she noticed the warm, homey scent filling the apartment.

"Wow, is that lasagna?" she asked, peering into the kitchen. Seeing the bubbling dish on the counter, she realized what Liam had done.

Liam turned to her, his face lighting up. "I thought I'd surprise you!" Despite his tiring day, he had found the energy to cook.

Sophie looked at Liam and then back at the lasagna. She wasn't hungry, but she recognized his thoughtful effort. Seeing his expectant expression, she decided to put aside her lack of appetite. "It's amazing, Liam," she said as she took her first bite.

Watching Sophie begin to eat, Liam felt a sense of satisfaction. He had wanted to do something nice for her, to make their evening a little bit special. Her compliment made the effort seem worthwhile.

Throughout the meal, they shared their day's experiences, their dreams, and even some of their worries. The atmosphere was relaxed and warm, a stark contrast to their day's hustle and bustle. Despite not being hungry, Sophie's decision to receive Liam's efforts graciously and gratefully had created a moment of emotional connection.

That evening, a simple meal became more than just food. It became nourishment for their connection, food for their butterfly.

Exercise: Generosity-in-Action Cards

Materials:
- Index cards or small pieces of paper
- A small box or container

Instructions:

1. Individually, each partner should brainstorm at least seven acts of generosity they'd like to do for the other to nurture the relationship or "feed the pet," one per day for a week. Color code it so you know whose is whose.

2. Once you've both prepared your cards, combine them and place them in the box.

3. Every morning, both partners should draw a card that corresponds to their color from the box, committing to fulfill that act of generosity by day's end.

4. At the conclusion of the week, take some time to reflect on the acts of generosity enacted. What was it like to consciously and intentionally nurture your connection and partner? What was it like to receive from your partner? Did you remember to be gracious? How can you work as a team to nurture your relationship even more moving forward? Repeat this activity every week until it becomes a habit.

The idea behind this challenge is to encourage daily acts of generosity regardless of what else is going on in your lives. It adds an element of surprise and excitement to your routine and allows you to express your love in new and creative ways. As you progress, you'll notice how these acts of generosity nourish and deepen your connection over time. Happy pet-feeding!

8

Differentiation

"I am rooted, but I flow."
– Virginia Woolf

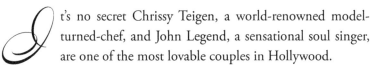t's no secret Chrissy Teigen, a world-renowned model-turned-chef, and John Legend, a sensational soul singer, are one of the most lovable couples in Hollywood.

In the early days of their relationship, Chrissy, with her unabashed candor and electric energy, was like a human espresso shot, keeping everyone on their toes. She was always the life of the party, known for her boisterous laughter and love of exotic cuisines. Her spontaneity and fervor for life had an infectious allure.

On the other side of the spectrum, John, with his soft-spoken demeanor and introspective nature, was more of a comforting, calming chamomile tea. His world revolved around soothing piano melodies and soul-stirring lyrics. He preferred quiet nights at home, listening to music or playing songs on his piano.

They appeared to have very little in common, yet there was palpable chemistry between them. The public, fascinated by their contrasting personalities, often wondered how lively Chrissy and tranquil John managed to build such a strong bond.

The secret to their harmonious union is their ability to appreciate differences and use them to their advantage. Chrissy's vivacious spirit added color to John's quieter world, while John's calming presence provided a safe haven for Chrissy from her bustling life.

They seem to have mastered the art of "complementary contrast." They teach us that sometimes the notes of a quiet piano can beautifully blend with the beats of an energetic drum. And so, Chrissy and John, an unlikely pair at first glance, have proven to the world that when love is the underlying melody, differences can create a beautiful harmony, bringing a delightful depth to the symphony of life.

* * *

Imagine a vast mosaic, a piece of art created by arranging many different colored tiles together. Each tile retains its unique color and shape, yet contributes to the unified, beautiful whole.

Differentiation, the fourth principle of the Butterfly Blueprint, refers to an individual's ability to maintain their sense of self within a relationship. It's about understanding and asserting your individuality and independence while simultaneously navigating and respecting interconnectedness. Differentiated people can engage in intimacy without losing their sense of self.

In his book, *Family Therapy in Clinical Practice* (1993), Dr. Murray Bowen, an American psychiatrist and a pioneer in the field of family therapy, defines differentiation as an individual's ability to distinguish their own thoughts and feelings from those of their family or group. A highly differentiated person can maintain their own beliefs and sense of self while staying emotionally connected to others, even in the face of conflict or disagreement. A less differentiated person, on the other hand, is more easily influenced and might become anxious in the face of disagreement and differences.

I often hear clients express frustration, saying, "What's the point in trying if I never get it right?" This sentiment shows an overreliance on feedback. Having the strength to show love regardless of the reaction or response you get from your partner is part of becoming differentiated. You need to have your own standards for what it means to be a good partner or parent and act on them regardless of the outcome. This is what it means to be a strong, differentiated, independent set of wings.

Imagine a butterfly attempting to fly with two identical sets of wings—either two left sets or two right sets, or four forewings or four hindwings. Not only would the butterfly's symmetry be thrown off, but its power, direction, and stability would be severely compromised. It would be completely dysfunctional. The beauty of a butterfly lies in the coordination of its differentiated, opposite, yet harmonious wings. In much the same way, each partner needs to have individual strength and balance for a relationship to work. Interdependence can only occur between two distinct entities.

The concept of embracing differences is underscored by the research of Dr. John Gottman and Nan Silver. They present an astonishing statistic that reinforces this idea: 69% of relationship conflict stems from perpetual, unresolvable problems that are rooted in fundamental differences in personality or lifestyle preferences (Gottman & Silver, 2015). That statistic should land like a thunderbolt! It's an earth-shaking revelation, to say the least! Recall all those countless moments you've fought about the silliest, smallest, pettiest things, like the classic "proper way to load the dishwasher" debate, where it seems like World War III could be sparked over whether the forks face up or down. A whopping 69% of those arguments are indeed futile and a complete waste of time and energy!

Picture a Venn diagram and the two outlier circle areas that depict the unsolvable differences between you and your partner. Hold both perspectives in your mind at once. Your partner has a right to be themselves as do you. You are each like one side of the coin with your own unique perspective.

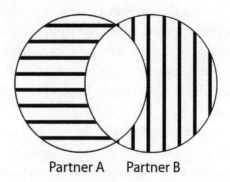

Partner A   Partner B

The shaded areas show how the two partners are opposites in many ways.

Many couples act more like lawyers than lovers when it comes to irreconcilable differences. This is where the *right-wrong* duality dilemma enters the scene. Each person brings their briefcase full of evidence that proves they are right and their partner is wrong. They provoke one another into escalating, heated debates until one of them shuts down and walks away, leaving no winners—just two frustrated, disconnected people who head to their respective corners until one of them breaks the ice; at which point, they both sweep the conflict under the rug until the next court battle is triggered.

The right-wrong duality debate becomes even more dire when character comes into play: "You're just a selfish…" and "You're such a miserable…" The "war" deteriorates to the level of who's good and who's bad as each partner assassinates the other's character with an onslaught of put-downs and demeaning, demoralizing, dehumanizing comments.

The more we get caught up in these endless egoistic arguments, the more we block ourselves from perceiving the true structure of reality, which includes both sides of the coin *and* the coin, both sets of wings *and* the butterfly, both individuals *and* the couple, or differentiation *and* wholeness.

The divisive part of the ego—the *"only for me"* approach—will do anything to protect whatever it deems precious just like Gollum's obsession with the "Ring" in *The Lord of the Rings*. Identity is one of the ego's most precious possessions, so the who's good and who's bad- or who's superior and who's inferior-based arguments get its full attention.

Recognizing differences or dualities is a powerful way to transcend the ego's desire for control. It shifts the focus from attempting to change your partner to appreciating your partner for who they are, separate from yourself. In doing so, it opens up space for both individuals to harmoniously coexist as their true selves.

* * *

Grant and Brenda are having trouble with differentiation. Grant is an extrovert, and Brenda is an introvert. They are getting caught up in whose personality is right and whose is wrong, whose is better and whose is worse.

Grant: "You know, I've been thinking about our social life. I'm an extrovert and I love being around people, but you, you're just not. You prefer being alone, and honestly, I think that's becoming a problem."

Brenda: "A problem? I can't help that I'm introverted, Grant. I find being around large groups really draining. It's just how I am."

Grant: "But don't you see? Being social is important. When we go out with friends, I feel alive. But you shut down or take days to recover. It's like you're avoiding living life to the fullest."

Brenda: "That's not fair! It's not wrong to feel overwhelmed in big crowds. You make it sound like I'm choosing to be this way. There's nothing wrong with wanting to spend time together, just the two of us. I wish you could understand that."

Grant: "I understand but I don't want to miss out just because you don't want to go out."

Brenda: "So, I'm the bad guy now because I don't enjoy parties like you do? Parties are chaotic and everybody's so superficial. It's like having a thousand friends on Facebook, they aren't *real* friends!"

Grant: "It's not about being the bad guy, Brenda. It's about what's right for us as a couple. How can this work when you're so against who I am?"

Brenda: "So now I'm against you? You're judging me! How are we ever going to find a middle ground? This is doomed!"

Grant: "Yeah, it feels like we're just incompatible. We're stuck."

* * *

So, what can you do with this 69% statistic? Do you have to accept the status quo, the apparent inevitability of oppositeness, and the huge gaps that surface as a result between you and your partner? Just because you and your partner don't see eye-to-eye on everything doesn't mean you can't manage the ways you differ from one another.

Remember, Mother Nature sets things up this way for a very good reason—so we will come to understand just how much *we need each other in order to maximize the abundance we can share*. We need the two sides of the coin, the 69% discrepancies and conflicts between us to guide us toward more meaningful, intimate, and fulfilling relationships, to point us in the right direction, like a compass. This will be further explained in the next chapter on unity.

In the meantime, differentiation calls for an elevated perspective, and the maturity to understand that acknowledging your partner's opposing viewpoint does not necessarily negate your own. Remember, a couple is made up of two different people by definition. It is through the process of differentiation that you can move beyond the impasses of right-wrong, good-bad, better-worse, and inferior-superior, and open yourselves up to a higher, shared goal. Instead of resigning yourselves to a life filled with "broken record" conflicts, you can strive for a connection that thrives *above* the differences. It's a challenging process to disentangle our own unique identities from those of our loved ones, and this is why it's great that we have three key practices to help us.

The first practice in attaining differentiation is to *acknowledge* the differences. Acknowledgment is like a respectful bow: it doesn't imply agreement or alignment. Nor is it about placating your partner or conforming. Instead, it's about simply recognizing and valuing your partner's opposing perspective without necessarily adopting it as your own.

Imagine a mirror placed under the bright sunlight. The light hits the mirror and is then reflected, illuminating something else, making it visible and radiant. Acknowledgment functions much like this mirror. When your partner displays a quality or shares a feeling that is different from your own, acknowledgment reflects the significance of that act back to them, highlighting its value and importance.

Opportunities to differentiate abound. When your partner is visibly upset or emotionally reactive, it's a clear sign that something that happened—or didn't happen—matters to them and impacts them, presenting you with a chance to shine the light of your conscious attention on how your partner is different and acknowledge it verbally.

Another unmistakable cue is the intuitive *uh-oh* moment—that gut feeling when you sense a disconnect or anticipate conflict. That sensation is your body's way of signaling, "Hey, pay attention; there's something related to differences happening here!" When your partner approaches with the dreaded, "We need to talk," and every fiber of your being resists because you're not one for verbal confrontations, remember: This is not just about a looming argument. It's an opening to recognize and acknowledge how you and your partner differ.

In the heat of the moment, you may be thinking that your partner just doesn't care and that you can't do anything right. These thoughts stem from deeper fears of abandonment and rejection. Instead of spiralling toward your dead end, you can pause and recognize the distinct ways you and your partner react, shifting from a confrontational attitude to an empathetic and understanding approach. This is internal work in the heart and mind.

When you are caught in the grip of a disagreement, it's crucial not to undermine or belittle your partner's traits *or* your own. Remember, both of you have unique histories and good reasons for showing up in the ways that you do.

Acknowledgment requires keen listening skills. Pay attention to your partner's perspectives without judging or interrupting (except maybe to reflect back what your partner is saying). Encourage your partner's interests, hobbies, and passions, even if they differ from your own, while maintaining balance over the long run. Instead of countering what your partner expresses with your own point of view, verbally acknowledge where they're coming from.

The second key practice as you make efforts to attain the principle of differentiation is to *accept*. Visualize a serene lake, its waters calm and undisturbed. Whether it's raindrops, fallen leaves, or tossed stones, the lake accepts them all, welcoming each without resistance. True acceptance in human interactions mirrors this tranquility and receptiveness, embracing diverse experiences, emotions, and perspectives without judgment.

Have you ever purchased furniture from the "as is" section at Ikea. These items come with their own flaws, but we accept them, knowing they have value and can fit perfectly into our homes. Your partner, much like that unique piece of furniture, may appear to have imperfections but is still irreplaceable in your shared life.

Acceptance also applies to oneself. Many people are extremely hard on themselves, prone to guilt, and unfairly beat themselves up for things that *everyone* does—just for being human like the rest of us. If you're one of those people, you may need to apply the practice of acceptance to *yourself*. You are irreplaceable and precious as you are, simply because you are. If you weren't good for something, you wouldn't exist. Remember, all of the life we perceive with our five senses is made up of dualities—plus and minus, good and bad—that goes for you too!

Nature doesn't make mistakes. Everything, and everybody, is good for something. Just as a fruit undergoes a natural ripening process, and we don't deem it defective when unripe, there is nothing wrong with you that isn't also a part of the shared human journey; remember, we're all in the same boat.

Acceptance is fundamentally internal work. Consider a partner who operates on a different schedule—perhaps they're perpetually late. True acceptance means you grasp this as a facet of their nature, without taking it personally, judging, or building up resentment. Accepting your partner is hard, nevertheless, because of the implications it has for you. Your partner's behavior (or lack thereof) inevitably impacts you and the connection between you.

Accepting your partner and yourself can make you feel like a fish out of water, as this means you'll be confronted more clearly with who *you* really are, including the disowned parts you might not be as familiar with. This can be uncomfortable, like looking directly into a mirror and not liking what you see. Accepting differences accentuates the contrasts between you. But this is part of the journey. It's okay. It's all part of the plan.

What shadowy part will you have to confront within yourself if you accept your partner's chronic lateness? Does this mean you have to spend your life sitting around, waiting and wondering? Or do you have options? What if your partner is messy or rigidly tidy? What surfaces inside you when you imagine accepting it?

What comes up inside when you imagine accepting *yourself* as you are? What are you afraid of? What if you choose not to wait around and wonder? What if you accept the part of you that wants to take charge of your life and assert yourself as a proactive player in your own story? What's the worst thing that could happen? Acceptance leads to a deeper emotional understanding of yourself, your partner, and the space that seems to divide the two of you.

Differences can feel threatening and uncomfortable, challenging your perception of yourself and disrupting your inner equilibrium. Acceptance is challenging since it demands that you confront the unfamiliar and the divergent head-on, pushing you outside of your comfort zone, shifting your center point.

For example, if you thrive on meticulous planning and you discover, over time, that your partner prefers more spontaneity, accepting your partner's spontaneity might mean fewer planned weekends and more unexpected adventures. While this could be exhilarating at times, it might also leave you feeling unsettled. The rhythm and predictability from planning that once provided a sense of security might be diminished. It might feel like you're losing something when what's actually happening is the reality of duality between you and your partner is being clarified.

Start off deciding it's time to really get to know and accept your partner. Try talking the way you did when you first met. Don't take things personally even though some of what your partner shares will inevitably impact you as described above because you are in a relationship and share various aspects of your lives. Just focus on absorbing who your partner *is*; be like a sponge and take it all in.

Often, the simplest questions can lead to the most profound discoveries about one another. Explore your partner's branches and roots, but not in a demanding, intrusive, digging kind of way. Rather, approach the conversation in a light-hearted, interested, curious, "chatting" kind of way.

Carve out an uninterrupted hour with your partner free from distractions. Take turns asking each other open-ended questions. Listen to the answers with an accepting attitude. The goal of the exercise is acceptance. Document your partner's answers by jotting them in a special journal or even creating a digital diary. Make it a monthly ritual to revisit and update your notes. Here are some questions to get you started:

1. What's your favorite food?

2. If you could spend a day as any animal, which would you choose and why?

3. What's something you've always wanted to learn or try?

4. If you had unlimited resources, what would be your dream job or project?

5. Which person in your life has influenced you the most?

6. What was a turning point in your life?

7. What's something that always makes you happy, no matter how bad your day was?

8. What's a fear or insecurity you haven't shared with many people?

9. What are your top five core values or beliefs?

10. How do you envision our relationship growing and evolving in the future?

When you're alone, reflect on what you've learned about the person you're in a relationship with! If you need more questions, google "conversation starters for couples." There are plenty online. Matthew and I did this on a recent date at a quaint little café in Cambridge. I learned some new things about him after over 13 years!

The third key practice for achieving differentiation in an interdependent relationship is to *accommodate*. Imagine a willow tree, its long, slender branches swaying and bending with every gust of wind, never breaking—like how the wings of a butterfly bend and "clap" together at various points. Instead of resisting, the willow tree adapts and moves with the forces around it. Accommodation in relationships mirrors the graceful flexibility of the willow, adjusting and making space for the needs, wishes, or imperfections of your partner, and the flow between you.

Accommodation involves a deliberate and active effort to adjust and adapt to your partner's needs, desires, and quirks. It's a conscious choice—a behavioral change meant to bridge the gaps that arise from your differences. When you aim to accommodate one another, you're shifting your personal boundaries to cultivate more harmony in the shared space.

Accommodating a perpetually late partner might see you tweaking your schedule or perhaps planning events a tad earlier. If your partner enjoys slow mornings, but you're an early bird—full of energy—consider using headphones to listen to the morning news, keeping things quiet for a bit longer.

Suppose you're someone who appreciates a well-organized space, but your partner tends to be more relaxed about leaving things around. Instead of insisting on constant tidiness, you could designate specific areas where things can be left out, like a particular chair or corner of the room for your partner's belongings.

* * *

Matthew and I make efforts to accommodate one another's wishes and desires. Matthew likes things to be tidy in the common areas of the house. I'm more comfortable with mess, but I make an effort to tidy up for him, even if it's just before he gets home (including making the bed!), just to please him. It's become a habit and I actually prefer things this way now too, although I never would have come to a place where I was motivated to tidy up more and can, therefore, enjoy my environment more if it wasn't for his desire and my willingness to serve his desire.

Matthew makes himself available to me when I ask for a "reservation." This is code for "I've had a rough day and I need you to be on the couch at 8 p.m. because I need affection and a cuddle." Matthew is naturally affectionate too; however, he benefits vicariously through my more frequent and direct requests, which he is much less likely to initiate. Together, we make space for each other's desires in these ways, accommodating them as though they were our own. Over time, this mutual accommodation has led us to a natural equilibrium, a homeostasis in which we both win.

* * *

It's important to notice that differentiation sometimes requires accommodation of yourself. Accommodating isn't just about prioritizing your partner's needs, but ensuring you take care of yourself and your own equally valuable and important set of wings too. For instance, if you're feeling overwhelmed or need some personal space, it's okay to declare a "me moment," however long it may be, even if it means your partner might feel disappointed. It took me years to learn the importance of accommodating myself in the equation of my own life.

* * *

I was in second year university and very depressed, missing my boyfriend who had moved back to Sweden when his parents divorced. I had been severely depressed in grade eleven too. I was never actively suicidal. I just didn't see a purpose for living or meaning in life. *Why are we here?* I wondered to myself. What's the point of life?

I was in university because that's what my parents had insisted upon, but when an old high school friend, Debra, came up with the idea to go to Australia on a backpacking adventure for a year, I jumped at the opportunity. This seemed like much more fun and had the potential for novelty and the unexpected. Maybe I would even find some answers to those big questions that were lurking in the shadows of my mind.

My parents didn't want me to go and tried to dissuade me. Deciding to go was one of the first independent steps I took in life for my own sake, to accommodate my adventurous spirit and need to get to know myself better and get more out of life.

My boyfriend returned to Canada as soon as he heard about the trip and tried to convince me to go to Sweden with him instead. He gave me an ultimatum. I had to choose between my trip and our relationship. I kept my word to my friend.

Debra and I dedicated nearly a year to working and saving, then embarked on our journey with stops in Seattle and Hong Kong. Our adventures were diverse and thrilling: We scuba-dived in Cairns, Australia; served drinks as bartenders at Bondi Beach; experienced the rush of tandem skydiving at Lake Taupo, New Zealand; and took the exhilarating plunge with bungee jumping in Queenstown, among many other escapades. While my quest was to feel alive and discover my true self, the journey took an unexpected turn for Debra, as she met her future husband. I, on the other hand, returned home alone about four-and-a-half months later, still feeling just as disconnected from myself as I did when we first set out.

Fast forward to age 37, about 15 years later, and I thought I was dying. After my near-death encounter with the 18-wheeler at the age of 25 in 1996, I had gone on with life, almost as though nothing had happened—continuing to seriously neglect myself. My life was devoted to raising my son the best I could, as both mom and dad. I returned to work about six months after the accident and completed my Master of Social Work degree in 2000.

By 2008, I was crawling up the stairs in the townhouse condo I had bought a few years earlier, suffering from chronic, debilitating back pain, gastro-intestinal issues, and severe depression—physical manifestations of my internal collapse. I hadn't gotten the rehabilitation I needed after the accident. I just didn't take my well-being seriously enough to make it a priority, apart from a couple of visits to various professionals and practicing yoga on my own at home.

It wasn't until 2008 that my life took a major turn toward self-care and self-accommodation. I was 37 years old. Years of accumulated physical and emotional scars demanded my attention. My life had been a desert for almost four decades, like a tree without roots, relatively devoid of self-awareness and self-compassion. I couldn't go on "pleasing, proving, perfecting, and performing," as Brené Brown outlines in her book *The Gifts of Imperfection* (2010). I went off work on disability and began the long, arduous process of self-discovery and healing in mind, body, and soul.

* * *

I've heard many women say, "I'm just a wife," or, "I'm just a mother," and "I've lost myself," in counseling sessions. The roles we adopt, such as provider, caregiver, peacekeeper, household manager, or problem solver, can impede the individual differentiation of each partner within the relationship.

Robin Norwood, in *Women Who Love Too Much* (1985), draws attention to the pitfalls of compulsive caretaking, a behavior prevalent among many women. This tendency stems from a deep-seated belief that their value is contingent upon their ability to care for others, often at the expense of their own needs and identity. Norwood cautions that this self-sacrificing pattern may not only diminish one's sense of self but also create imbalance in the relationship. It leads to a cycle where the more one partner does, the less the other feels the need to contribute, leading to an overfunctioning-underfunctioning dynamic that undermines the stability of the partnership.

Echoing a similar theme, Dr. Robert A. Glover's *No More Mr. Nice Guy* (2000) identifies a pattern in men who believe they need to please others to get what they want, often avoiding conflict, hiding flaws, and prioritizing others' needs over their own. Breaking free from the "nice guy syndrome" includes setting boundaries, prioritizing one's needs, and being honest with oneself. Cultivating personal integrity through self-accommodation is essential for establishing a harmonious balance within a relationship.

Balance, in essence, is the art of choosing when to accommodate yourself and when to accommodate your partner based on the situation at hand and the overall well-being of the relationship. Remember, a butterfly has two equally important sets of wings and they both need care so they can support the flight of the butterfly as a whole. The key is finding that equilibrium, together so you maximize the balance within each of you as well as between you, over time.

Learning how to accommodate yourself and your partner requires a healthy degree of independence. Being excessively dependent on your partner's perceptions, opinions, and reactions can hinder your ability to engage with the principles of the Butterfly Blueprint, especially differentiation. First discern what is right for the connection, then act, letting go of the outcome.

Learning to accommodate one another and ourselves is a big deal and should be celebrated when it happens. It isn't easy and it goes against our chocolate-love nature. Pat your partner (or yourself) on the back when either of you successfully accommodates the other! Great job!

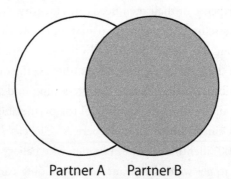

Partner A   Partner B

Partner A accommodates Partner B by putting Partner B first
(or B puts self first).

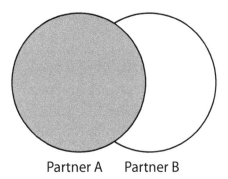

Partner A   Partner B

Partner B accommodates Partner A by putting Partner A first
(or A puts self first).

By consciously choosing to differentiate through acknowledgment, acceptance, and accommodation, you not only strengthen your bond. You evolve in your ability to love beyond the limits of a self-absorbed, chocolate-love approach. You are more honest and have more integrity. When both of you genuinely value your differences, your butterfly doesn't just fly; it *better-flies*! This improved and enriched "flight" is only possible when both sets of wings consciously harmonize through differentiation.

When *better-fly*ing is applied to a relationship, it means the couple can explore new heights, navigate life's winds more effectively, and experience a relationship that's dynamic, mutually enriching, and fulfilling. The *better-fly* doesn't just survive; it thrives, just like a couple that doesn't merely coexist but flourishes through the connection between them.

Differentiation doesn't imply that either partner needs to change. Brenda (from above) will continue to be introverted and Grant extroverted. These traits are integral to their respective personalities. Let's look at how Grant and Brenda turn things around when they approach their differences using acknowledgment, acceptance, and accommodation.

Grant: "Brenda, you know we've been talking a lot about how different we are, right?"

Brenda: "Oh, the whole Venn diagram thing from that book, *The Butterfly Blueprint*? Yeah, it's hard to accept. I guess we're different in ways we'll never change, but I still want to work on things and stay together."

Grant: "Exactly. Me too. Well, I've been thinking about our friends. I love socializing, but it's not the same when you're not there. I want to hang out with our friends *together*, as a couple."

Brenda (taking a deep breath): "I get that. It's not that I don't want to spend time with *you*. It's just so draining for me, especially when we go out on Fridays. I'm working on accommodating myself just the way I am. There's nothing wrong with the way I am."

Grant (nodding): "You're right! There's nothing wrong with me either! I don't want to force you to do anything, but I don't want to miss out either."

Brenda: "Agreed. Well, where there's a will, there's a way! I know you want to go to Scott's 40th next week. Maybe I can come for part of it and then head home. I might not be the life of the party, but I can at least show up, for your sake…and for our sake."

Grant (smiling): "That sounds perfect. We can watch that Netflix movie you mentioned too, maybe on Sunday, just the two of us. I'll even rub your feet! We just have to accept each other and make efforts to bridge the gaps ourselves so we don't keep growing apart."

Brenda: "It's a start. I think us being different can actually be a good thing. The contrast helps us get to know ourselves better, and we can push each other out of our comfort zones!"

Grant: "Totally. We have to make room for each other to be who we really are. It makes us stronger."

Discovering Differences: A Reflective Exercise for Couples

This exercise is an invitation to dive deeper into understanding yourself and your partner. As you engage in it, remember, differences aren't bad, they're the strokes of color that make your shared canvas come alive. They help you honor your unique identities while still celebrating your shared journey. There are infinite examples of differences like those listed below. Feel free to add others that resonate for you.

Instructions:

1. **Personal reflection:** Begin by taking a deep breath and centering yourself. Look through the following list and tick off the characteristic that resonates most deeply with your own self-perception. You might be torn, but pick the one that's *most* true for you. Don't think about it too much.

2. **Sharing and comparing:** Once both of you have completed the list, come together. Share your responses with one another, embracing the journey of mutual discovery. Add some context and detail to your choice as you talk. This is an opportunity to see where your characteristics and preferences merge and where they diverge. Feel free to put them on a Venn diagram, putting your similarities in the overlapping circle area and the differences in each of the outlier areas.

3. **Identifying differences:** As you share, you may find that your partner perceives you differently than you perceive yourself. That's the beauty of perspective! It's not about being right or wrong, or good or bad, but about acknowledging, accepting, and accommodating yourself and your

partner. Keep your map for reference and as a reminder. Add to it whenever you discover more differences.

1. Intimacy is…
   - ☐ Emotional connection
   - ☐ Sexual connection

2. Conflict resolution
   - ☐ Raise issues
   - ☐ Avoid conflict

3. Financial habits
   - ☐ Save
   - ☐ Spend

4. Planning
   - ☐ Planner
   - ☐ Spontaneous

5. Home is where…
   - ☐ Everything's in its place
   - ☐ I can relax if it's messy

6. Humor and playfulness
   - ☐ Let's crack jokes and laugh
   - ☐ Let's be serious and focus

7. I'm more in my….
   - ☐ Head (mind/thoughts)
   - ☐ Heart (body/feelings)

8. Punctuality
   - ☐ Don't be late
   - ☐ Don't rush

9. Risk-taking
   - ☐ Let go
   - ☐ Control

10. Predictability
    ☐ Enjoy adventure
    ☐ Enjoy routine

11. Parenting
    ☐ Consequences
    ☐ Talk things out

12. Sexual frequency
    ☐ Once a month
    ☐ Once a day

13. I think…
    ☐ Out loud
    ☐ In my head

14. Priorities
    ☐ Fun and leisure
    ☐ Responsibilities

15. Affection
    ☐ I'm touchy-feely
    ☐ No PDAs, please

9

Unity

"We are only as strong as we are united, as weak as we are divided."
– J.K. Rowling

I love romantic comedies. They're fun to watch, and they often illustrate lessons about relationships that I share with my clients. A while ago, I thought I would try my hand at writing my own screenplay about a couple grappling with a familiar duality dilemma. I'm still waiting for that blockbuster deal where Steven Spielberg buys my idea and we both win Oscars. But until that happens, here's my one-and-only attempt at writing a romcom....

Anna Miller and Jack Gray were not names one would come across in the headlines of tabloids or on the list of Hollywood's glitterati. Their fame came not from celebrity status but from their remarkable love story, which was the inspiration behind the blockbuster film *Together We Stand*. The couple became cherished and adored by millions worldwide.

Jack was a virtuoso violinist, renowned for his soulful performances, while Anna was a prodigy conductor whose passion for music matched Jack's, note for note. They found love in the symphony of music, bonding over their shared adoration for melodies and harmonies. However, each held a distinct philosophy. Jack believed in the power of individual performances, while Anna valued the unity of the orchestra, where each instrument, though individually less significant, together created a masterpiece.

This contrast of beliefs became a source of conflict, and the world watched as their love story unfolded amid tension and discord on the big screen. The turning point came when Jack was invited to perform a solo in an international concert. As he stood on the grand stage, his violin poised to begin, he found himself missing something. His notes, usually flowing like a river, felt disjointed and lackluster. In that moment, he realized the missing piece was the unity and harmony that had come from playing as part of an orchestra, under Anna's graceful direction.

As Anna watched Jack's performance, she could sense his inner turmoil. It reinforced her belief that a single note, no matter how beautifully played, could never match the richness and depth of a full orchestra. However, this also made her realize the importance of individuality in the larger picture. She understood that unity does not diminish individuality but enhances it by providing contrast and bringing out the best in each player.

This shared realization brought them closer than ever before. They understood that their love, much like an orchestra, was about harmonizing their individualities, not overshadowing either of them but bringing out the best in one another. From then on, their philosophy of putting unity above individuality echoed through every concert, every melody, and every note they played, earning them global recognition and adoration.

Ta-da! So, there you have it, Mr. Spielberg—you know where to reach me.

* * *

In a relationship, two individuals, each with their unique strengths, weaknesses, ideas, and dreams, come together to form a single unified entity. However, uniting as a couple doesn't require that you lose your individuality as a person. Instead, it necessitates a healthy balance of independence and dependence called *interdependence*.

Interdependence means each partner is comfortable being themselves, while they also acknowledge the value of mutual support and cooperation. It means making decisions and handling challenges together, yet respecting each other's autonomy and personal space. The principle of *unity* encourages partners to lean on each other, share responsibilities, and make concessions for the sake of the relationship—all while maintaining their individual identities.

In the same way that a caterpillar undergoes a stunning transformation into a butterfly inside a chrysalis, couples experience a similar metamorphosis when they consciously commit to their bond. This is where the magic of synergy in a relationship unfolds. Synergy occurs when the joint efforts of both partners create something new, like how alchemy transforms base medals into gold. Something new and extraordinary emerges; the whole is greater than the sum of its parts!

Just like each set of wings exists independently *and* is simultaneously part of a much greater whole organism—a butterfly—each partner is transformed and becomes their very best *through conscious connection*. Working together fulfills the ultimate purpose for both, which is to "fly!" What good is a set of wings if one cannot fly? The partners foster an environment between them, in their union, in which *each one self-actualizes through self-transcendence, in harmonious alignment with the other*.

This transformation isn't always comfortable or easy for a couple; it involves expanding (going outside comfort zones), stretching, and growing, like the metamorphosis of a caterpillar into a butterfly. Each partner transcends the limits of individuality and attains a higher level of human development *through* the relationship.

The essence of unity is beautifully symbolized by the Argentine tango, a dance that is unchoreographed and relies heavily on the connection between the two partners. It's a testament to the interdependence, synchronization, and harmony required in a relationship. In the tango, the dancers must *feel* each other and the music, moving in sync, responding to each other's cues. Each dance is one-of-a-kind, emerging from the synergy between the partners.

The hidden duality dilemma that gets in the way of attaining the principle of unity is the physical and mental disconnect between *you and me*, or self and other. Each partner brings a unique set of experiences, perspectives, and aspirations to the relationship. Identity is precious to each one and often presents blocks and obstacles in the pursuit of unity. When balance between partners seems to come at the expense of the balance within one or both individuals, uniting is a challenge.

People can get caught up in the pursuit of independence and self-expression. The desire to stand out and maintain one's uniqueness can sometimes cause disagreements. These conflicts might arise from differing opinions, diverging ways of dealing with things, or even in conflicting personal habits and tastes. Focusing on individual needs—the "me"—can overshadow the needs of the relationship—the "we"—making it harder to achieve unity.

This may sound contradictory, having just read Chapter Eight on the principle of differentiation. We need to attain both principles: differentiation and unity above the differences; a relationship requires a "you," a "me," and a "we." The key is to ask yourself, "Why?" Why am I exercising the practices of differentiation or unity in any given moment and set of circumstances? Am I aiming to build the body of the butterfly, the connection between us, in my actions? Or am I doing whatever I'm doing solely for my own benefit, at the expense of my partner and our relationship, or, conversely, solely for my partner's benefit at my own expense? *Every choice needs to take both partners and the connection into consideration.*

Part Two: The Butterfly

* * *

Matthew and I met online. We chatted back and forth for about a month before meeting for dinner and a movie. He came to Kitchener, where we met at Moose Winooski's for some food and then watched *Avatar* at a theater nearby. I remember being struck by the mix of mischief and magic in Matthew's eyes and agreed to meet again.

Matthew took me to Niagara Falls for our second date, where he presented me with a gold necklace with two interlocking hearts, one sparkly and one plain, which I still wear today. "I'm the sparkly one," I told him as I admired the beautiful necklace. "I had to hunt for this," he said as he put it around my neck.

As though it had been scripted, on our way back to the car, we had to jump over a chain-link fence. Matthew went first, and then my capris got caught on the fence as I was jumping over. Matthew was there, ready and waiting, and caught me as our bodies became aligned. He planted an unexpected kiss on my cheek as I recovered from my "fall."

Everyone in my family loved Matthew as they met him at different times throughout the following year. We took our two teenage children with us to meet the rest of his family in South Africa later that same year. It was during that three-week trip, we decided we enjoyed being together so much that we wanted to live together. We began searching for a place immediately upon our arrival back in Canada.

We bought a new build still under construction in Kitchener, and Matthew found a job only five minutes' drive away. Our lives were becoming more and more intertwined. Matthew moved into my condo first, and then, a month later, the three of us—my 18-year-old son included—moved into our brand-new home together. My son left to live in residence for his first year of university a month later.

While it all sounds like bunny rabbits and rainbows so far, no story is complete without a challenge, and we *did* have big problems too. Like with many blended families, the issue of divided loyalties came up for us. My son and I had disagreements and bickered like an old married couple at times. I had, after all, raised him by myself. Matthew hated to see me upset and would react behind the scenes, making it harder for me, as I was torn, caught in the middle of my two loves, my two favorite people.

Matthew sometimes felt the same way: torn between me and his daughter, who graduated from eighth grade the first year we were together. He made the difficult choice of relocating to Kitchener, about an hour and a half from where his daughter lived with her mom during her high school years. This wasn't easy for either of them.

While we both got along fine with each other's children on the surface of things, we each had a lot going on inside and couldn't talk about it without getting into heated arguments. I was often amazed by the stark contrast between Matthew's connection with his daughter and the relationship I had (or lack thereof) with my dad growing up. Matthew would buy her whatever her heart desired without her even needing to ask, and I sometimes felt envious of the father-daughter connection they shared. Matthew found this hard to understand or relate to since his dad had always been his best friend and his family was very close-knit.

Matthew and I never separated, but it wasn't always easy and we've even seen our own marriage counselor. The turning point for us was deciding that no matter what, we would stay together. We mattered, above the struggles. If our individual parenting styles were different, it would take more than those kinds of conflicts to tear us apart.

In the end, both our kids have benefitted from us being in a committed relationship. Once we agreed we didn't have to fix every last thing to stay together, we united in our mutual intention to make it work, for better or for worse, in sickness and in health…

* * *

The first key practice of unity is to *be intentional*—intentionally aiming toward a higher goal: the well-being of the connection. We so often say, "that's not what I intended," but the real question is, what was your intention? Unity raises us above the ego's divisive, chocolatey, "for me alone" interests and safeguards the harmony of equality. The *bilateral* you-me dilemma transforms and expands into an *equilateral* triangle—a new entity—when *both* partners aim themselves toward the benefit of the connection they share. Intention requires being *in tension* between the two sides of the coin, or the opposing forces in any given duality dilemma.

Intention is paramount in distinguishing the meaning and impact of an act, akin to how a surgeon's use of a knife for the purpose of healing contrasts with a murderer's use of a knife with harmful intent. The same act with opposite intentions transforms the meaning and impact of the act. An act without an aim is like a body without a soul; the purpose behind our actions is what truly defines them.

Engaging the prefrontal cortex plays a crucial role in the practice of intentionality. This part of the brain, responsible for thoughtful and deliberate calculation, requires a significant amount of energy to function. It's the center where we weigh options, consider consequences, and make constructive choices. By actively using this part of the brain, we can rise above impulsive reactions and make decisions that foster unity and harmony in our relationships.

Unity doesn't happen by chance; it requires conscious effort and deliberate action. Just as a rider on a horse can steer the horse to a particular destination rather than letting it gallop around wildly, intention prevents emotions from taking over and leading us into stuck arguments and dead ends. Like the mythical centaur with the upper body of a human and the lower body of a horse, we need harmony and balance between intellect and instinct. Intentionality is the guiding compass that helps us navigate through the complex dynamics of individuality (you and me) and directs us toward a unified, collaborative approach (we). It means acting purposefully, shifting from reactivity to proactivity, from reliving the past to creating the future.

When things get heated, we need to pause and choose words and actions deliberately. We need to be conscious of what we're doing and why or for whose benefit. In order to be intentional, a person needs to constantly ask themselves, "Why am I doing what I'm doing? What is my goal right now?" A second helpful follow-up question is "Is what I'm doing (how I'm showing up in the relationship) helping me to achieve that goal?"

Imagine a couple, Kofi and Amina, who often argue about household chores. Kofi feels overwhelmed and snaps at Amina for not helping enough. In a reactive mode, this leads to a heated argument. However, if Kofi chooses to be intentional, the approach changes. Before speaking, Kofi takes a moment to think, *What is my goal right now?* The goal is to have a more balanced distribution of chores. Then, Kofi thinks, *Is snapping at Amina going to help achieve this goal?* Realizing it won't, Kofi decides to calmly explain his feelings of being overwhelmed and asks for Amina's input on how they can better share household responsibilities. This intentional approach fosters constructive dialogue and cooperation rather than conflict.

One of the most significant steps a couple can take is to envision the kind of partnership they aspire to create. This shared vision acts as a guiding light or a North Star, helping partners navigate through the complexities of life together. It's about establishing a clear and mutual understanding of what each person desires and values in the relationship. By setting intentions and goals, couples can align their efforts and grow together in a direction that resonates with both.

The Venn diagram can serve as a valuable tool to depict a shared vision—your intentions—for your relationship. Begin by setting aside quiet, undisturbed time for a frank and honest discussion about your aspirations for your "butterfly." Prepare for this conversation by reflecting on what you hope to achieve in different facets of your life and relationship. Refer back to the exercise at the end of

Chapter Eight on differentiation for relevant topics. When you've gathered your thoughts, talk about your vision together:

1. Start with the common ground, those topics you see eye-to-eye on, and write down your shared vision in the overlapping circle area of the Venn diagram. For example, "We're aligned when it comes to how we want to raise our children and the values we want to instill in them."

2. Next, tackle those checklist items in which you have different perspectives and priorities that are complementary. Write down the complementary differences in the outlier circle areas but just next to the overlapping circle area. These differences do not divide you. They are not problematic. For example, one of you likes routine and the other one enjoys adventure. Life is enriched for both of you because of this difference in your personalities.

3. Now identify those differences that collide and conflict. Consider how you might be able to aim yourselves to become aligned. Where is the wiggle room in your imaginations to move forward together when it comes to these discrepancies? What are your learning curves and growing edges that you wish to lean into to become a united team going forward? For example, you may have discrepancies in sexual desire. The one with less desire might be willing to set up a sexual intimacy date once a month during which the focus is on mutual pleasure through touch without necessarily having to engage in intercourse (more will be said about this in Chapter Eleven on intimacy). The other partner may be willing to set up an emotional intimacy date once a month during which the focus is on talking and sharing without sex coming into play.

4. Finally, write down those differences that seem irreconcilable in the outer edges of the outlier circle areas of the Venn diagram—the farthest away from the overlapping area—for each of you. These are the hot-button topics that lead to heated arguments when you try to address them. It may seem as though these are unresolvable without solutions. For example, one of you might want to make a budget and have much more control over how money is spent, whereas the other one is unwilling to abide by this approach. Just identify these differences. Don't argue. Just write them down.

Completing the Venn diagram exercise with your shared vision at its center and individual differences in the outlier areas provides a visual representation of your relationship's unique dynamic. It's like taking inventory of your relationship or doing a reality check. It shows you where things are working well, where you are both working to improve things, and where things remain difficult. It's all good. As you move forward, let this diagram serve as a living document, evolving as you do, and guiding you in nurturing a relationship that is both fulfilling and enduring.

The second key practice in attaining the principle of unity is to *exert in the labor of love*, which essentially means being willing to sacrifice, yield, and make concessions for the sake of harmony in your shared place—the overlapping circle area in the Venn diagram. While the practice of accommodating from Chapter Eight means making efforts to go along with your partner's wishes, exerting in the labor of love takes things a step further by conceding in order to add more harmony.

The phrase "labor of love" applies to various scenarios where effort and sacrifice are made out of love and affection. It could be nurturing a dream, building a home, caring for a family member, or working toward a shared goal with a partner. These actions, fueled by love, often involve a personal cost, be it time, energy, or resources, but are undertaken willingly. The driving force behind a labor of love is the deep satisfaction and fulfillment derived from the act itself and the joy of achieving the desired outcome. It's a testament to the power of love in inspiring individuals to go above and beyond, enriching both their lives and the lives of those they care for.

The concept of a labor of love can be seen in various aspects of life where individuals willingly endure challenges and make sacrifices to achieve their goals. The Latin word for sacrifice is sacrificium. This term combines "sacer" (sacred) and "facere" (to make), literally meaning "to make sacred." Think of women who willingly become pregnant, knowing full well the pain of childbirth and the many sleepless nights to come, but choose to have a baby anyways, drawn by love for the yet unborn child. The birth is literally a *labor* of love.

Consider students who invest years in education, often undergoing stress and fatigue, to attain the qualifications needed for their dream careers. Similarly, athletes subject themselves to rigorous training routines, enduring physical strain and exhaustion, in pursuit of peak performance and competitive success. Musicians dedicate countless hours to practice, honing their skills and perfecting their craft, often at the expense of leisure time and comfort. Examples abound, and why shouldn't your relationship deserve this kind of loving sacrifice too?

It's important to distinguish between the labor of love and the labor of guilt. The labor of guilt is rooted in fear, obligation, or the feeling that one "ought" to do something. Like the saying goes, "Don't *should* on anyone," including yourself. This can lead to resentment and a sense of being trapped, which is harmful for everyone involved. Guilt-tripping either yourself or your partner can create an imbalanced dynamic where one partner consistently overextends at the cost of their own well-being and the overall health of the connection.

Marshall Rosenberg's concept of "emotional liberation" from *Nonviolent Communication* (2015) offers a pathway out of the labor of guilt. It involves shifting from emotional slavery, where you feel responsible for other people's happiness and act out of obligation, to a state of emotional liberation, where you act out of compassion and care. In this liberated state, you don't lose yourself to meet others' needs out of fear, guilt, or shame. Instead, you acknowledge your own needs and feelings while also respecting those of your partner. This balance allows for actions that are fulfilling to both you and your partner, fostering a healthier, more equal relationship.

Triggers are perfect opportunities to exert in the labor of love. Couples often face difficulties when intense emotions, disproportionate to the present situation, arise as echoes from unresolved childhood trauma or wounds from previous relationships. Partners say things like, "It's not fair! I'm not his mother! Why do I have to pay for her mistakes?" or "I don't get it. I've never given her any reason to believe I would cheat! I'm not like her ex!" By choosing not to take these reactions personally and, instead, consciously working together to confront and heal these past pains as a team, the couple forms a powerful united front. This collaboration acts as an effective shock absorber, significantly reducing the impact of these emotional echoes.

It can be meaningful to share with your partner when you're actively engaging in the labor of love for the betterment of your bond. This isn't about seeking praise or laying a guilt trip; it's about building awareness. Letting your partner know that your efforts are rooted in the love you share and your dedication to your mutual goal to build an interdependent relationship can add opportunities for appreciation and deepen trust.

"We suffer to get well. We surrender to win. We die to live. We give it away to keep it"—here, Richard Rohr's paradoxical wisdom beautifully conveys the journey of conscious relationship-building. "Suffering," "surrendering," "dying," and "giving it away" all enrich relationships in unexpected ways. We don't lose. We gain from all of the above. When both partners make conscious efforts to exert in the labor of love for the sake of their relationship, they benefit exponentially, as they each receive so much back in return from the shared bond they build together.

Conflict also provides opportunity to engage in the labor of love. Without conflict, there isn't a place to show your willingness to stretch outside your personal comfort zones for the betterment of the relationship, to yield and make sacrifices. When both partners exert a joint effort, the labor of love can bridge and heal any gaps. This approach requires understanding that each time you set aside a personal preference or position, it's not a loss or defeat but a valuable investment in the unity you both depend on. It's money in the bank!

It's about consciously filling the *space* between you with love, turning it into a rich and abundant *place* of shared connection. This is like making regular deposits into a bank account. Sure, you don't get to spend the money right away. This is a sacrifice. But, over time, the deposits build up, providing you with the freedom to spend it as desired, without the constraints that come with repaying a loan. Investing in your relationship through continuous, conscious effort creates an abundant emotional account from which both of you can draw as needed, without all those exorbitant interest charges!

* * *

Matthew and I have engaged in the labor of love when it comes to our finances. He is all about saving for retirement, whereas I am more interested in enjoying life day to day. I have conceded to his desires by saving on a monthly basis as well as putting larger lump-sum amounts of money into a retirement account over the years. He has also conceded to my desires by going along with the trips I book and organize as well as the renovations I spearhead.

The great news is that each of our lives is better for it! Even though we make concessions for one another that can "hurt" in the moment, we end up with more in the long run. I will now be able to retire one day. And when we're enjoying fun in the sun, Matthew often says, "Thanks for organizing this!"

We enhance each other's lives and get the best of both worlds—the best of each other—through mutual concessions. We both end up with more! If Matthew is a blue circle in the Venn diagram and my circle is red, together, in the shared place between us, we create *purple*! Purple—the new life that emerges through synergy—gives both of us more than either of us could have ever achieved on our own, either as solid blue or solid red. Purple, flutters like a butterfly, lifting us both up on the wings of love!

* * *

Imagine a recurring issue or argument in your relationship. It could be something as basic as a disagreement over household chores or something more foundational, like managing finances. The next time this issue arises, consider how you can engage in the labor of love for the sake of maintaining and building unity in your relationship. Decide to show up with a different attitude—perhaps with more patience, openness, or willingness to put yourself in your partner's shoes. Don't shy away from the discomfort. Make an effort. Exert yourself. Sacrifice. Have your partner's back. Honor your relationship. Lead the way toward more balance and harmony in the connection between you! But make sure you're doing it out of love!

Keep a reminder of your decision to engage in the labor of love—a note on your phone, a written journal entry, a sticky-note on your computer, or even a symbolic object in your purse or pocket. Make a conscious effort to remind yourself of your decision to persevere through discomfort for the sake of your relationship. (Remember, the key is not to cause yourself pain on purpose—we're not talking about purposeless suffering or masochism here—but to endure difficulties when necessary for the greater good of the relationship.) Pull out the symbol when things get heated to help you calm down and remember to aim for your North Star, your purple butterfly—the connection between you and your partner that means so much to you.

At times, the labor of love must be directed toward oneself, toward nurturing one's own set of wings. This becomes particularly important if you feel that your partner is not prioritizing you, leaving you feeling unimportant or sidelined in their eyes. Often, this external feeling of being undervalued mirrors an internal struggle where you also find it challenging to prioritize your own needs. It's a common tendency to focus on the perceived shortcomings or neglect of a partner, seeing them as the "bad guy," while simultaneously overlooking the parallel issue of self-neglect. If caring for yourself or being cared for makes you feel guilty, you might need to work on laboring on behalf of your own set of wings. This isn't selfish when you do it for the sake of the relationship, for the benefit of the butterfly as a whole.

The third key practice regarding unity is to *be committed*. So many couples refer to their relationships as "rollercoasters." Commitment implies being there for each other through the inevitable ups and the downs, the highs and the lows, during the storms of disagreement, misunderstanding, and external pressures—not because it's always fun—but because your relationship is worth it in the long run. Like all the other dualities we've touched upon throughout this book, you can't know the ups without the downs or have the highs without the lows since they are two sides of a coin. It is normal and natural to oscillate between connection and it's opposite, disconnection, as well as balance and it's opposite, imbalance, over the course of time. Remaining committed through both means you are a friend in need and not just a fair-weather friend!

The story of Christopher (Superman) and Dana Reeve is a poignant example of commitment and strength in the face of adversity. After Christopher's tragic horseback riding accident left him paralyzed, their relationship was put to the ultimate test. Yet, instead of succumbing to despair, they showed extraordinary resilience and dedication to each other. They even worked together to advocate for spinal cord research and improve the quality of life for people with disabilities. Dana's unwavering support for Christopher until his death in 2004 is widely regarded as an inspiring example of strength, love, and commitment in the face of life's most daunting challenges.

In the whirlwind of a wedding, couples stand before each other to exchange vows publicly and make promises that are meant to bind them over time in sickness and in health, for better or for worse. The big day is charged with emotion and significance, yet as the months and years go by, these vows can fade into the background, sometimes forgotten amid the routine of daily life; we become complacent and take each other for granted.

Commitment extends far beyond the vows exchanged on a wedding day; it's an ongoing daily practice. To keep the essence of your mutual commitment alive, you can engage in commitment rituals. These rituals are purposeful activities that partners can incorporate into their lives as a means to reinvigorate their vows. By conducting commitment rituals at least twice a year, couples create opportunities to remind themselves of and celebrate the deep devotion they share.

At the beginning of each year, plan at least two dates dedicated to reflecting on the past half-year's highs and lows and evaluating how your commitment to each other played a role in navigating these experiences. How did you highlight and celebrate the good times? How did you stick together during the challenging times? What did you learn about the value of commitment through your experiences?

Make sure your commitment rituals are special. Pick a special place and time. Come prepared as you were on your wedding day or on the day you decided to be a couple and share a home, children, and finances. Reflect on what commitment means to you. Do you value it more or less? How do you demonstrate it to your partner? In what ways would you like to demonstrate it differently in the future? How do you want to honor the connection between you and your partner through the good times and the bad moving forward?

* * *

Andrew and Amber had been married for eight years and had two young children and a third on the way. They sought counseling to address their escalating arguments, which never seemed to get resolved. After the conflict, they would stop communicating for several days, except for the bare essentials related to the kids, until one of them would eventually break the ice. They would then sweep the issue under the rug until the next time. Their most recent disagreement was about whether or not to purchase a larger home, which had reached a boiling point, leaving them both drained and unwilling to back down.

"I can't believe you're so willing to put our family's future at risk," Andrew said, his voice shaking with frustration. "You're always so impulsive and short-sighted. You don't think about the long-term consequences!"

Amber bristled at the accusation. "I am not short-sighted! I'm thinking about our family's future, and that means getting a bigger house. We can't stay in this shoebox forever!"

"But at what cost?!" Andrew shot back. "What happens if we take on a bigger mortgage, and then something happens? What if one of us loses our job or we have unexpected expenses? We'll be stuck, unable to pay our bills and provide for our kids!"

"I understand the risks, Andrew. I'm not stupid," Amber said through gritted teeth. "But we can't just live in fear all the time. Sometimes we have to take a chance to get what we want in life!"

"But why take unnecessary risks?!" Andrew retorted. "We're comfortable here. We have everything we need. We're finally getting a little bit ahead financially. Why mess with that?!"

"Because we need it!" Amber said, her voice rising. "I want our family to have more space, more freedom, more opportunities. Is that so wrong?!"

The tension in the room was palpable as they continued to argue, each refusing to budge (lacking *in-tension*). It was clear their priorities were at odds, and finding a compromise seemed impossible.

Andrew and Amber are a perfect example of nature's opposing dualities in a relationship. Andrew wants to play it safe and hold steady financially, enjoying what they have, making sure they're not house-poor. His perspective is completely justifiable. He feels the weight of being the primary breadwinner and doesn't want to jeopardize the family's newfound financial security.

On the other hand, Amber wants to plan for the future and invest in a bigger property, making sure there's ample room for their growing family. They can afford it if they choose to, without going into too much debt. Investing in a bigger house could also prove to be a long-term financial benefit. Sure, their mortgage will be bigger, but everyone has a mortgage, so what difference does that make? She's comfortable with the risks involved. Amber's position also makes perfect sense and is easily understandable.

Andrew and Amber exhibit two equally valid, seemingly opposing viewpoints on the surface: *play it safe* or *take a risk*, to make it simple. The contrasts between these two approaches trigger each of them in different ways. Andrew feels threatened and anxious, and Amber feels powerless and unheard. They start to see one another as the bad guy and get caught up in a tug-of-war, each trying to bend the other to get their own way. They're entering the outlier areas on the Venn diagram, feeling more like two separate, divided sets of wings rather than a single whole butterfly. They're conflicting and out of balance with each other—or so it seems on the surface.

When we delve a little deeper, we can see that Andrew and Amber may not be as disconnected as they feel. They share a life together, including finances, a home, and beloved children. They both want what's best for their family. They just have different opinions about how that looks moving forward.

In their next counseling session, Andrew and Amber began to explore their respective viewpoints more carefully. It was evident neither of them was trying to harm or oppose the other. They both loved their family deeply and were attempting to ensure the best future for their children. They decided to approach the conversation with the principle of unity in mind. They both made efforts to be intentional as they continued the discussion of this hot-button issue:

Amber took a deep breath. "Andrew, I understand you're concerned about our financial stability. I admire that about you. But sometimes I feel that if we're too cautious, we're gonna miss out! We've been living in the same space for so long—with the new baby coming—I'm afraid we'll feel even more cramped."

Andrew nodded. "I get where you're coming from, Amber. I'm just trying to protect us. But I understand that life is about taking some calculated risks too."

Amber sighed. "What if we meet in the middle? Maybe we don't need the most expensive house on the market, but something a bit bigger."

Andrew pondered this. "Yeah, if we wait a year or so, we can save up more for the down payment too."

Amber smiled. "Well, at least that's not a 'no!' At least, we're talking about it constructively. The important thing is, whatever happens, we'll get through it together."

In this dialogue, Amber and Andrew demonstrate a willingness to bend and find middle ground, without either of them completely compromising their core beliefs. The conflict opens the door for deeper understanding, connection, and effective interdependence.

Exercise: Our Covenant

Creating a "shared garden" agreement can be a significant step for a couple to express their united intention to cherish and nurture their relationship. Envision this shared space as a garden you're cultivating together. Both partners need to aspire to be "good gardeners" and tend the whole garden together, not just one's own flowers and veggies. Write yours in a way that resonates with both of you, treating this agreement as a living testament to your commitment to each other. A commitment is especially important for those times when you feel disconnected and alienated as a couple. It serves as a much-needed reminder of your shared goal and the higher purpose for the "worse" and "sickness" times. Here's an example:

We are now building a place between us—a shared garden.
We enter with a new approach, with a focus on our connection.
Afterall, this is going to be our shared place, our beloved garden.
We open our hearts and minds to each other, including our differences.
We each have our own preferences about what to plant and that's okay.
We tell each other what we would enjoy most in a perfect garden.
After the initial excitement of planting, we nurture our garden daily.
We fertilize each other's plants, fruits, and bushes as well as our own.
We take responsibility for the garden, learning new skills as needed.
We weed and care for it diligently, knowing it will die if we don't.
We protect each other's sense of safety and enjoyment in the garden.
We strive to be good examples, leading and following when necessary.
We avoid complaints and instead create positive vibes so it thrives.
We proactively tend to it with careful thought and effort—not neglect.
When storms come, we remember we don't have to be in control.
We huddle together, trusting in our connection to get us through.
When the time comes, we enjoy the fruits of our labor together.

10

Wholeness

"To be ourselves causes us to be exiled by many others, and yet to comply with what others want causes us to be exiled from ourselves."
– Clarissa Pinkola Estés

The film *Jerry Maguire* tells a powerful story of Jerry's self-discovery and journey to wholeness. Jerry (Tom Cruise), a successful but spiritually unfulfilled sports agent, finds himself confronted with his inadequacy and seeks a sense of authenticity in his life. His personal growth is catalyzed by his relationship with Dorothy (Renée Zellweger), a single mother and accountant who becomes a beacon of sincerity in his superficial life.

Early in the film, Dorothy sees something in Jerry that he doesn't see in himself. Upon hearing Jerry's impassioned mission statement (to introduce more care and ethics into the sports management business), which cost him his job and most of his clients, she declares, "I love him for the man he wants to be. I love him for the man he almost is."

Jerry struggles in his efforts to become a whole, balanced person. He is caught between the lure of his old life of money and fame and the promise of a new one filled with authenticity and meaningful relationships. The turning point comes in Dorothy's loving confrontation with Jerry when she says, "You are the last person I would ever set you up with," reminding Jerry that his growth was still a work in progress.

Slowly, Jerry starts to embrace the values Dorothy embodies—compassion, care, and integrity. His relationship with Dorothy and his commitment to his sole remaining client, Rod, starts to change him. When Rod says to Jerry in a pivotal scene, "Help me help you," Jerry is reminded of the value of authentic connection—of helping and complementing one another in this challenging world, whether within a couple or in business relationships.

This culminates in the famous scene where Jerry blurts out to Dorothy, "You complete me!" This line expresses his acknowledgment of Dorothy's profound influence on his life. He sees the man he wants to be mirrored in Dorothy's eyes—a man driven not by the chase of success but by authentic relationships and love. Through his relationship with Dorothy, Jerry gets to know himself more deeply, leading him to become a more integrated, whole person.

* * *

Wholeness is the sixth principle in the Butterfly Blueprint. In the intertwining lives of a couple, each partner's unique attributes and experiences are like distinct colors and textures in a tapestry. The individual strands, representing their hopes, challenges, and journeys, are woven together through the course of their relationship. This weaving process creates a tapestry that is richer and more complex than any single strand could offer.

Human beings need each other in order to become whole. Clinical pastoral counselor, Harville Hendrix beautifully describes the complementary dynamics of partner selection in his book *Getting the Love You Want* (1988). He suggests people are drawn to partners who have the blueprint for the unfinished business of their childhood. We don't just choose someone we're attracted to and share interests with; we are unconsciously or instinctively drawn to individuals who offer us the potential to heal and grow, to integrate our "shadow" parts as discussed in Chapter Three.

Carl Jung said attaining wholeness does not come from eliminating or cutting off from our inner parts, but instead by *integrating* our contraries, our opposing light and shadow sides. It is through the acknowledgment and acceptance of our entire selves—our fears, doubts, and weaknesses as well as our strengths and virtues—that we become complete human beings. He also said, "The best political, social, and spiritual work we can do is to withdraw the projection of our shadow onto others."

Society and culture often propagate the notion of individualism, suggesting that completeness and wholeness are attainable solely through self-reliance and personal achievements. This message is perpetuated through various mediums such as media narratives, self-help literature, and even educational systems. However, this perspective overlooks a fundamental aspect of human nature: our unavoidable interdependence.

The truth is, humans are social beings, fundamentally wired for connection, a trait deeply ingrained in our biology and psychology. From an evolutionary perspective, our ancestors relied on social bonds for survival. The work of John Bowlby and Mary Ainsworth demonstrates the importance of early social bonds in shaping our ability to form healthy relationships later in life. These bonds with parents or caregivers influence one's sense of security and attachment style. Studies show that social connections are essential for mental and physical health. Social isolation has been linked to increased risks of depression, anxiety, and physical health problems.

A person's growth, learning, and emotional well-being are deeply intertwined with their relationships. The journey to wholeness is not a solitary endeavor but a collaborative process, enriched and supported by our interactions and bonds with others. It's through these shared experiences and mutual support that we truly find completeness.

The *internal-external* duality dilemma that gets in the way of wholeness takes us back to Chapter Three, where we explored the two worlds of roots and branches, the seen and unseen dimensions of life. This dichotomy, where the concealed inner world contrasts with the revealed external world, poses a significant challenge in our pursuit of wholeness, intimacy, and effective interdependence. We often feel imbalance and a lack of harmony between these two worlds.

A common response to a lack of inner balance is to try to alter the external environment. We mistakenly believe that by changing external circumstances or people around us, we can achieve internal peace and wholeness. This approach overlooks the complex interplay between our internal state and the external world. By focusing solely on external modifications, we may ignore the deeper, internal roots of our challenges. This tendency to externalize the quest for inner harmony hinders one's journey toward true wholeness and interconnectedness.

Human perception is inherently limited, confined to the realm of what is immediately knowable regarding both ourselves and others. The roots, representing our innermost thoughts, feelings, and desires, often remain hidden, yet they significantly influence our external actions and interactions, symbolized by the branches. Even in the world of branches, perception through the five senses is distorted and skewed, largely based on a person's past experiences.

Within this dichotomy, we often find ourselves entangled in conflicts that stem from limited perception. Misinterpretations and misunderstandings frequently lead to arguments and disconnection. We form assumptions, theories, evaluations, conclusions, judgments, conjectures, hypotheses, inferences, interpretations, and even diagnoses, all of which capture only a small piece of the larger truth.

In this landscape of limited perception, we often fall into the trap of assuming that we know "The Truth," placing ourselves at the center of reality rather than human connection. There's a tendency to view one's own beliefs and understandings as absolute, discounting what lies outside our personal experience as either false or irrelevant. This stance negates the reality of duality. By assuming the role of the sole arbiter of the truth, we fail to acknowledge the multifaceted nature of human experience and the richness that differing perspectives bring to one's understanding of the world.

It's very interesting to ponder the fact that you cannot see your own face or the mole on your back. So much of communication happens through facial expression, especially the eyes, and we have no way of witnessing this part of ourselves except with the assistance of a mirror. We live our lives from the inside looking out. It's like we have half of the picture of reality. We lack the opposing vantage point: from the outside looking in.

In a relationship, your partner is that mirror, reflecting profound truths about your roots, enabling your growth toward a more complete version of yourself. The reflections and feedback from your partner offer valuable insights into your own character and behaviors, highlighting not only areas for improvement but also positive aspects of yourself that you may not fully recognize or appreciate. This dynamic underscores the significance of relationships in our lives—they are not merely about companionship but also serve as vital instruments for self-discovery and personal development.

* * *

As touched on in Chapter Six, I was in an abusive relationship as a young woman. Believe it or not, despite the fact that my life was a living hell at that time and I thought it would never end, I look back on it now and understand why things had to happen that way. The truth is, I didn't know myself, my preferences, or my deep-seated feelings of worthlessness at the time. Unknowingly, I sought out someone who reflected this extremely negative self-image back at me by treating me...well...like shit.

In a way, Jeff's treatment of me was unconsciously familiar since a shadowy part of me felt it was all I deserved. If he hadn't mirrored my low self-image back to me so I could perceive it from the outside in, I would never have been able to get to know this wounded part of me that so desperately needed attention and care in order to heal and grow.

As awful as things were in this relationship, they needed to be that way in order for me to evolve as a person and become more whole as my own set of wings. Growing pains are not fun, but they are necessary if we wish to become all that we were meant to be, our best selves.

I want to clarify that in no way am I suggesting or implying that I deserved to be abused or mistreated (or that anyone does). The relationship with Jeff, as painful as it was, acted as a catalyst for me to confront and address the parts of myself that felt unworthy and undeserving. It was through this difficult experience that I began to recognize and heal the wounded aspects of my relationship with myself.

* * *

The magical mirror works both ways. It's the overlapping circle area in the Venn diagram or the body of the butterfly that connects the two sets of wings. The middle ground is like the two-way mirror in police interrogation rooms. From the concealed vantage point behind the reflective window, it's easy to scrutinize your partner's actions and behaviors, analyze their motivations, and identify their underlying reasons—all while protecting yourself from the same scrutiny. We like to dissect our partners' internal landscapes but are not open to the same introspection or critique regarding our own.

I see this a lot in counseling. It can be so much easier when one's partner is on the hot seat, being asked all the questions. In a truly balanced and healthy relationship, partners must be willing to step in front of the mirror themselves. The willingness to be seen and to see yourself through your partner's eyes, so you can understand and expand your self-image to include those dark, shadowy figures, is key in achieving wholeness.

It's crucial to recognize the importance of turning inward and doing our own inner work rather than trying to change our partners. Self-correction is about acknowledging that real change and balance come from within. Instead of bending the external world to fit our desires or ease our discomforts, we need to bravely confront our own shadows and shortcomings.

This inward journey involves critically examining our motivations, biases, and emotional reactions. It's a process of uncovering and understanding the deeper aspects of our psyche that influence our behavior and relationships. Embracing this path of self-awareness and self-correction is fundamental in attaining a state of wholeness. The difficulty of this work underscores the importance of adhering to three key practices.

The first key practice in attaining the principle of wholeness is to *face your fears*. Rather than looking in the two-way mirror of reality from a concealed vantage point and scrutinizing your partner, switch the mirror around so you are using it to see inside yourself. Face the core fears that fuel your self-protective defenses and block connection with your partner.

While facing fears is a key practice in achieving wholeness, as Gavin de Becker explains in *The Gift of Fear* (1997), it's important to recognize that not all fears should be confronted for growth. Sometimes, listening to our instinctual fear is crucial for safety. This natural response can alert us to real dangers, guiding us to avoid potential harm. In the context of relationships, while it's valuable to explore and face internal fears that hinder connection, we must also be discerning about external threats. This discernment helps us navigate situations where our safety, rather than our emotional growth, is the priority.

Facing your fears involves confronting a more subtle adversary: the human ego that seeks the benefit of itself alone. The ego protects itself in myriad ways and lives in constant fear for itself and its own identity. It harbors fears related to its status, particularly the concern that it is not superior, or, conversely, that it is actually inferior. This apprehension stems from the ego's deep-rooted need to maintain a certain self-image and sense of importance.

In counseling sessions, it's common for couples to describe their arguments using language that indicates power imbalances and power struggles. These descriptions vary widely, with partners feeling like a child, maid, servant, employee, assistant, subordinate, doormat, second-class citizen, slave, sidekick, or even the low man on the totem pole. Some express feeling like they're treated as a punching bag within the relationship. Often, partners will remark, "We're both stubborn," indicating a mutual resistance to feeling lesser or subordinate to the other.

The presence of Dark Triad personality traits—Machiavellianism, psychopathy, and narcissism—introduces significant challenges in relationships. As noted by Dr. Anna Machin, individuals with these traits (as well as sadism) often exhibit aggressive, callous, manipulative, and exploitative behaviors. They prioritize their own benefits at the cost of others, lack empathy, and are self-centered. Such personalities tend to devalue others to elevate themselves, manifesting self-glorifying attitudes. These individuals are adept at looking after "number one," often to the detriment of those around them (Machin, 2022). Again, I hate to say it but we're all in the same boat, albeit to different degrees. Who hasn't ever behaved in a manipulative way? We all have.

Pia Mellody, known for her work in the fields of addiction and codependency, discusses grandiosity as one of the manifestations of developmental immaturity, stemming from childhood trauma or neglect. In her framework, grandiosity is seen as a defense mechanism that individuals use to compensate for deep-seated feelings of inadequacy, worthlessness, or shame. It's essentially an exaggerated sense of superiority or an inflated self-concept. This grandiose self-image can lead to behaviors such as arrogance, entitlement, and a lack of empathy (or contempt) for others. In relationships, it can manifest as a need for control, a tendency to devalue others, or an inability to see others as equals. Grandiosity is often seen as the opposite of the "wounded inner child"—while the wounded inner child feels vulnerable and insufficient, the grandiose or "adaptive inner child" feels superior and omnipotent (Mellody, 1989).

The fear of being inferior can trigger a range of responses aimed at compensating for or masking perceived shortcomings, shame, and weakness. This fear manifests through comparison and competition, where individuals measure themselves against others, experience jealousy and envy, and feel the need to constantly prove their own value.

The wounded inner child also fears being judged or criticized by others, as this can be seen as clear evidence of inferiority. This can lead to a reluctance to admit mistakes or consider feedback. Instead, individuals might become defensive, aggressive, or dismissive in order to protect their ego.

Additionally, the fear of inferiority can make it challenging to genuinely celebrate others' successes or be empathetic toward their struggles, as the ego might interpret these situations as reflections of its own shortcomings.

The underlying theme in facing our fears and attaining wholeness is the human longing to feel good enough and the fear of not meeting this mark. Whether it's through the defenses of grandiosity or the vulnerabilities of the wounded inner child, individuals strive to protect their self-worth and avoid the sting of inferiority. Either way, the ego lives in fear for itself, thereby limiting one's capacity to attain wholeness since wholeness is achieved through relationship. Let's see how facing fear helps Alex and Jamie avoid an argument.

One day, Alex was sitting at the kitchen table, going through bills when fear cropped up behind the scenes. Jamie was on the couch, scrolling on her phone as tension quickly filled the room.

Alex (voice raised): "You know, Jamie, I feel like everything's on me. Groceries, bills, kids' schedules…I'm tired."

Jamie (defensively, looking up from her phone): "I do lots around here! I worked late the last three nights, and I'm just taking a break. Can I not have a moment of peace?"

Alex (voice shaking, a whirl of emotions): "It's not about you, Jamie. I'm drowning over here and you don't even seem to notice or care!"

Jamie (feeling accused, voice rising): "Well, maybe you should say you need help instead of just constantly complaining! I can't read your mind."

Both simmer in silence, hearts racing, thoughts racing faster. The attack-defend duality dilemma is up and running. Alex remembers to slow down and aim for connection.

Alex (voice softening, realization dawning): "Wait, Jamie…This isn't about the bills or groceries…I'm scared."

Jamie (confused and curious): "Wait, scared of what?"

Alex (taking a deep breath, eyes misty, voice cracking): "When I was twelve, after that accident with my sister, my parents split. I…I always felt like it was my fault. If I had just been more responsible, maybe they'd still be together. It's like if I don't stay on top of everything, if I let anything slip, we could fall apart…I could lose you."

Jamie (pulled closer, any traces of frustration melting away): "Oh, Alex…I'll never leave you."

Alex: (feeling insecure): "I know it sounds crazy. I just can't help but think if I'm not in control, everything will come crashing down. It's all on me. That's probably why I can't ever seem to sit still or relax."

Jamie (gently): "It actually makes sense. Thanks for telling me. That sheds some new light on things."

Alex (admitting his fear): "It's so hard to ask for help. I've always had to handle everything. It's scary to think of letting go."

Jamie reaches out, taking Alex's hands as new understanding bridges the gap between them.

The next time you find yourself in that all-too-familiar downward spiral with your partner, take a moment to pause. Resist the temptation to get caught up in the surface-level details, the content, the process, or the branches. Instead, dare to go deeper inside and do your inner work.

Understand the importance of the hidden world of roots. You may find painful physiological sensations inside. You may find dark, demeaning thoughts and beliefs about yourself. You might find a numbness that will also likely lead you back to fear.

This is the time to face your fears, to dare to look into the mirror your partner is holding up for you. You might not like what you see, and that's okay. You might feel a surge of emotion, and that's okay too. You might discover beliefs that protect you from having to *feel* fear at all. Facing these lost, scared parts of yourself is key in attaining the relationship you desire. This work isn't easy. But the rewards are immense. As you take this brave step, ask yourself: *What am I afraid of?* Here are some common fears that often surface in relationships. Which ones ring true for you? Write your related reflections in a journal.

1. Fear of rejection or abandonment

2. Fear of not being good enough

3. Fear of losing control

4. Fear of vulnerability

5. Fear of being hurt or betrayed

6. Fear of conflict or confrontation

7. Fear of change

8. Fear of dependency, weakness, or neediness

9. Fear of loneliness or being alone

10. Fear of losing oneself or one's personal identity

11. Fear of failure

12. Fear of powerlessness and helplessness

13. Fear of intimacy or emotional closeness

14. Fear of criticism or judgment

15. Fear of disappointing others

16. Fear of the unknown or uncertainty

17. Fear of repeating past mistakes or patterns

18. Fear of commitment

19. Fear of losing independence or freedom

20. Fear of not being able to meet a partner's needs or expectations

Each of these fears, when brought into the light of consciousness, can be understood and healed. As long as we avoid our fears, they run the show from behind the scenes. Having the courage to face our fears when that false alarm bell rings and a shadowy figure appears is necessary in the journey toward wholeness. We are not as "in control" and invulnerable as we'd like to think.

In relationships, the real fear that needs addressing is the erosion of connection between the partners. This connection is like an umbilical cord that nourishes a fetus— it's essential and life-giving. Disconnection breeds illness while connection fosters the restoration of well-being. In our modern world, just as a poor Wi-Fi connection disrupts our digital interactions, a lack of internal, emotional connection between partners leads to issues and suffering.

Carl Jung said, "The first half of life is devoted to forming a healthy ego, the second half is going inward and letting go of it." This inward journey is not about discarding the ego but about understanding its role and transcending its limitations, allowing for a more holistic and authentic expression of the self. It's a transformative process that opens the door to greater emotional depth, richer relationships, and a more profound sense of connection with oneself and the world.

The second practice in attaining wholeness in an interdependent relationship is to *integrate your parts*. According to the Internal Family Systems (IFS) model of psychotherapy, developed by Dr. Richard Schwartz in the 1980s, each of us contains a multitude of inner parts that contribute to our personality. It's like we have lots of relationships going on within ourselves. It's common for some parts to take dominant roles while others might be more submissive. Some may be inclined to attack while others defend, and some parts might think they are right and discount the perspective of other internal parts as wrong. Notice the parts inside of us get caught up in the same duality dilemmas we face in our couples.

The conflicts we experience within ourselves often reflect the dynamics of our interactions with our partners. The push and pull of opposing forces that we experience internally among our various psychological parts are similarly reflected in our external relationships. In much the same way we strive for harmony with our significant others, it is equally important to cultivate a sense of inner peace. Achieving inner balance is crucial, as it not only enhances our personal well-being but also the health of our relationships.

This is where integration comes into play. It involves recognizing and accepting all parts of ourselves, even those shadowy ones we might prefer to ignore or deny. These are the parts that worry about being inferior because they are either "too much" or "not enough." Integration involves bringing these parts into our awareness and understanding their roles and motivations as well as their intentions and internal impact. Rather than allowing these parts to operate in isolation from behind the scenes, we seek to bring them into conscious dialogue with each other, fostering a sense of wholeness within ourselves.

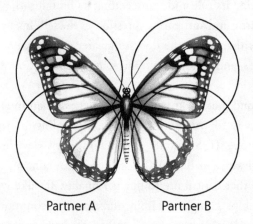

Partner A   Partner B

Each partner does their inner work by integrating their internal and external worlds, their own roots and branches, their inner shadowy parts with their conscious parts, building strength and balance between their own two wings.

Dr. Richard Schwartz's research on family systems shows that when we integrate these parts, we develop a sense of self that acts as a confident, compassionate leader or wise adult within us. This self can mediate between the parts, bringing inner balance. The prefrontal cortex plays a vital role in this process, aiding in the regulation and integration of these internal parts, thereby fostering greater self-understanding, self-acceptance, and ultimately, a more balanced and satisfying relationship since the internal and external worlds are mirrors of each other; our relationships are as healthy and whole as we are individually.

* * *

When my son was an infant, I moved back in with my parents since I didn't have the means to care for either of us at the time. One of my mother's friends came to visit and told me about her counselor and how special she was. She gave me her name and number, and I reached out right away.

This counselor was attentive, warm, and present. I could feel her attunement to me and was amazed by the thoughtful questions she asked. She convinced me to join her group for abused women and I did so without hesitation. I attended the stage one and stage two groups and then, one evening, in stage three, when sitting in the circle of women who had become like sisters to me, things got very real, very fast.

All eyes were on us as the counselor and I debated. The group listened, riveted, as the two of us got into a challenging, emotionally intense debate. I was full of questions and resisted the answers she was giving as we fired back and forth. Suddenly, tears welled up in my eyes, and overwhelmed, I covered my face with my hands, blurting out, "Because I hate myself!" In a rush of emotion, I jumped up and fled the room, desperately seeking a place to hide from my own shame.

This was the evening when I first encountered my shadow side, the fearful, dark part of me that lurked within, telling me I was no good—a "worthless piece of shit," as I used to say. Years of emotional isolation had left me bereft of a sense of self. All that was there, inside, as we discovered that evening, was a belief that I *felt* so bad because *I was* bad.

* * *

Childhood Emotional Neglect (CEN), a concept explored in depth in Jonice Webb's *Running on Empty* (2012), sheds light on how many aspects of our inner selves—especially those that feel unloved or insufficiently acknowledged—are formed. CEN occurs when a child's emotional needs are consistently overlooked, ignored, or invalidated. This neglect doesn't necessarily stem from a lack of love but often from a lack of understanding or awareness from caregivers. These neglected parts—while unseen—shape our reactions, relationships, and self-perception in adulthood. We tend to find ourselves marrying into the relational dynamics modelled for us by our mothers and fathers.

The Still Face Experiment, conducted by Dr. Edward Tronick in the 1970s, demonstrated the impact of emotional responsiveness on infant development. In the experiment, mothers interacted normally with their babies, then abruptly switched to a still, unresponsive expression. The babies initially tried to engage their mothers, but when their efforts failed, they showed signs of distress, such as fussing, crying, and turning away. Upon resuming normal interaction, the mothers were able to quickly re-establish the connection, highlighting the importance of emotional responsiveness and attunement in relationships.

Collectively, those parts of ourselves that didn't get what they needed when we were young are referred to as the "inner child." It's important to give your wounded inner child a "seat at the table" in the journey toward wholeness. This underscores the significance of acknowledging, listening to, and validating the needs and feelings of your inner child. While we cannot change what happened in the past, we can change *the impact* of what happened *in the present* by making room in our hearts and minds for all our parts to grow and develop.

Cultivating this relationship with your inner child can be truly transformative, and one potent way to do this is to approach and engage with your inner child as you would a dear friend or beloved child. Indeed, a striking contrast often exists between the ways we treat ourselves versus those we deeply care about. Internal integration is about bridging this disparity. Why wouldn't your inner child be equally deserving of the same kind, compassionate, patient treatment, and understanding you give your loved ones?

Imagine treating your inner child with the same care, gentleness, and consideration you'd extend to your closest friend or your cherished child. The same kind words, the same patient understanding, the same warm comfort—they all belong to your inner child as much as to your loved ones. By honoring this connection and offering such kindness to your inner self, you nurture a more compassionate, understanding relationship with your own being. This, in turn, contributes to a healthier, more fulfilling relationship with your partner.

In contrast to the nurturing approach to healing the inner child, Terrence Real, in his book about male depression, entitled *I Don't Want to Talk About It* (1977), refers to the concept of the "harsh" or "adaptive" inner child, as previously mentioned with reference to Pia Mellody. The harsh child represents a defensive persona that many men (or more masculine partners) develop in response to emotional pain. This persona is marked by grandiosity, toughness, and emotional withdrawal, serving as a shield against perceived weakness.

Real suggests that the harsh child is a form of overcompensation for the suppressed "wounded child"—the part that is vulnerable and hurt. Rather than addressing their emotional pain, men often internalize it, leading to the development of this harsh, protective self. While this may initially serve as a defense mechanism, it can become counterproductive, manifesting in destructive behavior, strained relationships, and further contributing to the cycle of depression.

The harsh child prevents men from seeking help or expressing their emotions healthily, often leading to a breakdown in meaningful relationships. Real emphasizes the importance of acknowledging this harsh child and integrating it in a healthy way. He advocates for understanding and confronting societal norms around male emotional expression, encouraging men to embrace a more emotionally open and authentic way of being (Real, 1997).

* * *

As the third child out of four, I had learned to get straight As and clean the house as a way to get attention and approval. I was an over-achiever, a type-A personality. I would win the track and field race, even if the stress of it meant I vomited all over the track and got a migraine afterwards. I had to prove my worth and be perfect. In fact, I used to get in trouble in elementary school for putting my hand up too often to answer all the teacher's questions. I *over*-participated!

I read a lot of Nathaniel Branden's books, like *The Six Pillars of Self-Esteem* and *How to Raise Your Self-Esteem*, during my personal healing journey. While studying Branden's works, the stark contrast between how I would berate myself and then be kind and helpful to others crystalized in my mind. I started to think, *That's not fair! If they deserve love and compassion, then so do I!!*

Branden recommended keeping a photo of your younger self—maybe four or five years old—with you, so I did. In the photo, I am looking directly into the camera. I see my eyes. I see my innocence. I see a beloved little girl, a child worth loving.

Whenever I would think to myself, *You should be ashamed of yourself!* I'd pull that picture out of my wallet and tears would start streaming down my face. I had always loved children growing up; I had wanted a baby as early as I could remember, to love and be loved by. That innocent four-year-old in the photo certainly didn't deserve to be talked to that way.

I learned to be very protective of her. I became her Mama Bear. I not only learned to be kind to her and compassionate but to listen to her too. Though she was in need of lots of TLC, she could be a ton of fun too. I got back in touch with the childlike life force that had been buried underneath my depression for so many years, even decades. Integrating with her helped me to heal and grow.

* * *

The third practice of attaining wholeness is to consciously *complement your partner*. Change your approach to the overlapping circle area, the shared place, by consciously complementing (not complimenting) rather than conflicting with your partner. Conflict turns the overlapping circle area in the Venn diagram into an empty space. Complementation transforms it into a shared—dare I say *sacred*—place, a sanctuary. Complementing your partner involves actively seeking ways to enhance and enrich their strengths and support their weaknesses. Navigating moments of tension or conflict requires conscious effort to shift from a fearful mindset of self-preservation and self-protection to one of connection-protection and mutual growth.

This is the time to engage in the transformation of motivation as discussed in the Introduction to Part Two. In order to complement one's partner, one has to bridge the gap consciously, like in the allegory of the long spoons when the people fed one another across the table instead of trying to feed themselves (and subsequently starving).

Embracing the transformation of motivation strategy sometimes requires a "fake it till you make it" approach, where deliberate effort gradually evolves into more natural behavior over time. This concept aligns with the neurological principle that "what fires together wires together"—meaning, as you consciously practice new behaviors, like attending to the middle ground between you and your partner, these actions start forming new neural pathways in the brain. Over time, this conscious effort becomes second nature, as consistent practice solidifies these behaviors into your brain's wiring. By repeatedly bridging the gaps between you and your partner, even when it feels forced initially, these acts of understanding and empathy eventually become an integral part of your relationship dynamic.

In the heat of the moment, taking a few deep breaths can help to calm the nervous system and create a mental space before responding. Taking a pause can prevent reactive, destructive behaviors and foster more thoughtful interactions. Instead of focusing on your fear for self or crafting a rebuttal, try to genuinely understand your partner's perspective. Listen without interrupting. Try to put yourself in your partner's shoes.

To complement means to complete, balance, harmonize or perfect. While giving into fear for self leads to escalating conflict, holding onto the connection between you provides hope and strength. This requires that you find that place in your heart and mind where you know that you love your partner. This doesn't mean you have to agree with your partner. It just means not turning your partner into an enemy and remembering the life you share. From this place, once you've reconnected to it, then you can move forward in an inclusive way with mutual understanding toward your shared goal: emotional and physical intimacy. Let's see how Jordan and Lara succeeded to complement one another as they navigated their relationships with Lara's parents.

Jordan and Lisa found themselves at a crossroads when it came to handling Lara's parents who were loving but overly involved in their lives, especially since the arrival of their second child. Lara, ever the diplomat, struggled to set boundaries out of fear that she might hurt her parents' feelings. Her natural inclination to avoid conflict was at odds with her nuclear family's need for personal space. Jordan, on the other hand, possessed a straightforward approach, unafraid to voice concerns but often lacking the gentle touch Lara's parents responded to best. The tension reached a peak during a family gathering where differing parenting advice became the topic of heated debate, leaving Lara torn between her parents and her role as a mother.

In the quiet aftermath, Jordan recognized the emotional toll the situation had taken on Lara. Acknowledging his partner's struggle to mediate between her parents and their family's autonomy, he proposed a solution that played to both their strengths. Jordan suggested they host a casual dinner, offering a neutral space where Lara could gently express their need for more independence while he supported her through direct, yet respectful conversation. They decided to make Sunday brunch a special, weekly event when Lara's parents were explicitly welcomed, providing a structured opportunity for extended family bonding without infringing on the couple's need for more day-to-day privacy and autonomy.

This approach allowed Lara to lead with her empathetic under-standing, softened by Jordan's assertiveness, ensuring their message was conveyed firmly but kindly. It also honored the role of grand-parents and the support of extended family, reinforcing the value of these relationships while setting respectful boundaries.

Complementing each other in a relationship serves as a power-ful catalyst for individual and collective growth, leading to a greater sense of wholeness and interdependence. When partners actively recognize and utilize each other's strengths while offering support in areas of weakness, they create a dynamic of mutual empowerment. In this nurturing environment, partners not only grow together but also evolve into more well-rounded individuals, each contributing to the other's journey toward a fuller, more balanced interdepen-dent existence.

Partner A   Partner B

By consciously complementing each other, the partners in a couple create a nurturing environment that brings forth new life, growth, strength, and peace in the shared place between them. It helps them become more whole inside and out.

The journey toward wholeness cannot be embarked upon in isolation. Contrary to the popular belief in self-sufficiency, we gain the deepest understanding of ourselves through our relationships. Romantic relationships act as mini-laboratories in which we learn about ourselves and how to truly connect. Replacing reactivity with radical responsibility is key.

This includes listening to and valuing feedback from our partners, and stepping away from the duality dilemmas that can trap us in unproductive cycles. Recognizing that reality includes both sides of every "coin" and that a harmonious balance between them is essential, allows us to grow toward wholeness. In this process, our partners are not adversaries but gifts, aiding us in our quest to become complete, integrated individuals within the framework of mutually enriching relationships.

The Complementary Strengths Exercise

Start by individually reflecting on your own strengths, particularly those you bring to the relationship. Think about qualities like empathy, organization, creativity, or humor. Take about five minutes to write these down.

Next, share your lists with each other. As you listen to your partner, acknowledge and appreciate their strengths. This step is about recognizing and valuing what each of you contributes to the relationship.

Then, switch to writing down the strengths you see in your partner. Try to identify the qualities in them that you admire and that positively impact your relationship. Share these with each other and discuss why you value these strengths.

Now, brainstorm together how you can utilize and enhance these strengths in your day-to-day life as a couple. For instance, if one of you is great at planning, consider taking the lead on organizing trips. If the other is a good communicator, they might handle family discussions or social planning.

Finally, come up with a concrete plan. Agree on specific actions and situations where you can apply these strengths. Schedule check-ins, once a month, to discuss how this exercise is influencing your relationship and make adjustments as needed.

11

Intimacy

"Real intimacy is born precisely out of the impact of your human imperfection with mine and how we both handle that maddening, endearing, challenging, and creative collision."

– Terrence Real

rank and Simone had known each other since college. An energetic young man and a vivacious young woman, they had fallen in love after meeting in a study group. Over the years, their lives intertwined into the beautiful mess life often is, leading to a home and two lovely children. Their bond was strong, their love evident. But as the years passed, they found themselves grappling with a delicate, unspoken issue—a disparity in their levels of sexual desire.

Frank, still as sprightly and passionate as in his youth, found himself yearning for the physical intimacy they once shared. His desire for Simone hadn't faded; it was as if he was still that 21-old college kid, smitten with her smile.

However, Simone, having been through two pregnancies and the rigors of motherhood, found her desire dampened, her energy sapped. A once-enthusiastic athlete, she had always been comfortable in her skin. But pregnancy and childbirth had changed her body in ways she was still coming to terms with. Her sexual desire had taken a backseat. She longed to want Frank the way she used to but often found her desire falling short.

Frank was wrestling with his own worries. He misinterpreted Simone's lack of initiation and enthusiasm as a sign of her dwindling attraction to him—as rejection. He started questioning his allure and his ability to satisfy her. Doubts began to creep into his mind, the silence around their situation adding to his insecurity. Would it be this way forever?

Physical affection, once a natural aspect of their relationship, had turned into complicated territory. Simone worried that any show of affection might lead Frank to expect sex, something she often wasn't inclined toward. Consequently, this concern made her increasingly hesitant to offer hugs and kisses as time went on.

Despite the complexities, Simone didn't shy away from physical intimacy altogether. There were times she'd comply with Frank's advances, not out of desire but out of fear—fear that Frank might feel neglected, and fear his eye would wander or he might end up seeking satisfaction elsewhere. But the Nike approach of "just doing it" was taking a toll on her, making her feel detached, disingenuous, and resentful. They had entered into what Doctors Peggy J. Kleinplatz and A. Dana Menard call the "sexual death spiral"—a decline in sexual satisfaction leads to engaging in sex out of commitment or guilt rather than desire, resulting in even less desire, increased conflict, and emotional distance over time (Kleinplatz & Menard, 2020).

Their once-intimate relationship had hit a rough patch, their silent struggle creating a widening chasm between them. The longing in Frank's eyes met the fear in Simone's, a silent acknowledgment of the issue at hand. They knew they had to navigate the tumultuous waters together but they didn't know how or where to start.

* * *

Intimacy refers to a close, familiar, and unique bond between two individuals. It is often characterized by a deep level of understanding, trust, and emotional connection. Intimacy can be expressed emotionally, physically, intellectually, experientially, and spiritually.

During mating, butterflies exhibit a courtship ritual where the male often performs a series of visual or chemical displays to attract the female. This can include fluttering around her in a dance-like manner or releasing pheromones, making it a multi-sensory experience. Once the female accepts the male, they mate, showcasing the nuanced ways in which these creatures communicate and connect to propagate their species.

Intimacy and sex, while related, are fundamentally distinct aspects of human relationships. Intimacy encompasses a deep emotional and psychological connection that goes beyond the physical. Sex primarily refers to a physical act that *can* be an expression of intimacy, but sex can also occur in the absence of intimacy with a focus on pleasure or reproduction. Sex is neither the sole method nor a necessary condition for an intimate connection. Couples who no longer have sex, for whatever reason, can still be intimate.

Intimacy isn't driven by hormones but is instead a conscious act where both partners converge with deliberate attention and intention. Sex—when infused with intimacy—transcends its physical dimensions, becoming a deeply erotic experience that is enriched and intensified by the internal emotional and mental closeness shared between partners.

Sexual intimacy and emotional connection are deeply related. For couples who enjoy a strong emotional bond, the depth of emotional closeness and understanding plays a pivotal role in their sense of fulfillment, with sexual intimacy being a complementary component rather than a defining one.

In contrast, when couples feel emotionally disconnected, the role of sexual intimacy becomes much more prominent. In such situations, sexual dissatisfaction often becomes a major point of contention, acting as a heightened representation of the overall health of their relationship. Sexual problems often indicate deeper unresolved issues and unfulfilled needs, becoming a primary focus in the concerns about the relationship.

Intimacy issues often stem from a common issue involving the mind-body connection where one partner views a strong sex life as a path to emotional closeness, while the other requires emotional intimacy to spark sexual desire. The partner desiring more sexual intimacy may experience heightened emotions and a sense of deeper bonding after a sexual encounter. In contrast, the other partner needs affection, open communication, and emotional connection as a prerequisite to fully engage in and enjoy their sexual relationship.

Sexual intimacy, while being a natural and integral part of romantic relationships, often remains an awkward topic of conversation among couples, especially when it comes to erectile dysfunction, premature ejaculation, and pain during intercourse. One primary reason is societal and cultural conditioning that frames sex as something to be experienced, not discussed. Another stumbling block is the fear of judgment, rejection, or hurting one's partner's feelings. The deeply personal nature of sexual desires and experience can make individuals apprehensive about sharing, for fear their partner might judge them as abnormal or reject them entirely.

Compounding these fears is a general lack of language to articulate sexual desires or concerns. The lack of open dialogue about sex in many circles can leave individuals at a loss for words when trying to express their feelings or needs. Insecurities about body image, for example, can be difficult to discuss. When individuals are uncomfortable in their own skin, they may be reluctant to draw attention to their bodies by discussing their sexual needs or desires. The sensitivity of the topic and the potential for disagreements to escalate into full-blown conflicts lead to avoidance. Finally, past experiences of sexual trauma or negative encounters can make discussions about sex particularly distressing and challenging to navigate.

People believe intimacy should be easy and natural; however, as relationships progress, it becomes evident that maintaining a sexual connection requires intention, active engagement, and effort. Intimacy represents the culmination of the foundational principles in the Butterfly Blueprint, including surrender, equality, generosity, differentiation, unity, and wholeness. These principles and the corresponding eighteen practices provide additional guidance for deepening intimate bonds.

1. **Surrender** in intimacy means taking off your armor, letting your guard down.

2. **Equality** ensures that both partners feel respected and valued during emotionally or sexually intimate interactions.

3. **Generosity** extends to the bedroom, where it translates into a willingness to nurture an intimate connection.

4. **Differentiation** is crucial for maintaining a sense of self within the sexual relationship, allowing each partner to express their unique desires and related boundaries.

5. **Unity** represents the aim or intention to build emotional and sexual intimacy as a team.

6. **Wholeness** means creating a balanced and fulfilling sexual bond for each partner that complements the overall relationship.

In the scope of human relationships, a couple's bond stands out as the most intimate connection one can experience. This is because, unlike other relationships, it involves a deep emotional, physical, and even spiritual convergence. Partners not only share daily life and its challenges but also dreams, feelings, and beliefs. This holistic interweaving of the roots and branches of two lives creates a unique bond unparalleled in depth and intensity.

The relationship between a mother and her baby is undeniably profound and significant but remains fundamentally different from a romantic partnership. The mother-baby relationship is primarily nurturing and protective in nature. In a couple's bond, there is a mutual sharing of vulnerabilities, dreams, and beliefs, and a two-way exchange of support and understanding. This interdependence between two mature individuals is distinct in depth and intensity.

Esther Perel, a therapist and international speaker, delves deep into the nuances of love and desire in her acclaimed work *Mating in Captivity* (2006). She touches on the intriguing paradox in which love seeks closeness, but desire often craves distance. As Perel insightfully expresses, we cannot desire what we already have. The security and routine acts of caretaking within relationships can unintentionally diminish erotic vitality. Differentiation, as explored in Chapter Eight, therefore, plays a key role in maintaining sexual desire over time.

Perel also claims that confidence, in many ways, is the most magnetic of all attractions. Confidence is not merely about physical allure or flirtatious gestures but is deeply rooted in how one feels about themselves. When individuals are balanced in various aspects of their lives—whether through diet, regular exercise, fulfillment in work, connection with nature, immersion in music, enjoyment of friends, or participation in sports—they exude a vital life force. This energy isn't directly linked to sexuality, but helps make a person feel sexy and attractive to others. The vibrancy of truly living becomes an irresistible force, enhancing the depth and quality of intimacy with one's partner (Howes, 2021).

The *close-distant* duality dilemma significantly disrupts our capacity for intimacy. We gravitate toward our partners when they delight us, driven by a chocolatey desire for emotional and sexual pleasure. Longing for the warmth of connection pulls us close. On the flip side, fear, sparked by the prospect of emotional pain pushes us away from our partners, prompts us to erect barriers, seek distance or "space," and prioritize self-protection. Caught in this push-pull dynamic, we oscillate between experiencing the connection as "too much"—and push it away—or "not enough"—and pull it closer. This tug-of-war between our longing for pleasurable connection and our dread of painful connection renders intimacy a challenging, often elusive pursuit which is why it's great that we have three practices to guide us.

The first key practice for achieving intimacy in your relationship is to *talk*. *Just talk*. Talking doesn't necessarily imply decision-making, expectations, obligations, nor does it have to translate into behavior. In essence, it's about sharing your internal landscape—the parts you can articulate through words, images, metaphors, and the like, like you did when you first met. Communication can be like communion, a sacred sharing that deepens the bond and nurtures the heart.

In your discussions, avoid getting trapped in a cycle of debating whose perspective is right or wrong, which is like bouncing between the separate edges of your Venn diagram. Instead, strive to stay centered in the shared space, where both of you exist together. Focus on expressing your own feelings and ideas, and when you do refer to your partner's words, let it be to mirror back what you've understood, demonstrating active listening. Take turns in the roles of talker and listener, or make it clear when you're sharing from within verses listening. This approach keeps the conversation within the overlapping area of the diagram, emphasizing inclusion and nurturing the trust that forms the foundation of your intimate connection.

Our bodies speak much louder than the words we say. Studies show that the huge majority of communication is nonverbal. When you practice talking with your partner, pay particular awareness to the messages your body is saying, intentionally or not. Even not moving a muscle speaks volumes. Body language that fosters a sense of safety and trust typically involves positioning your torso so it's facing toward your partner, maintaining gentle eye contact, and displaying a pleasant, relaxed facial expression. Practice in the mirror. Your face does not likely appear the way you think it does since you usually don't see it while you're having a conversation. The widespread use of Zoom and similar platforms since the onset of COVID-19 has confronted many of us with our body language as others see it, offering a new perspective on how we present ourselves from the outside in.

Think back to the early stages of dating, when the primary aim was simply to get to know each other. During those moments, conversations were characteristically open and exploratory, often marked by smiles, laughter, and curiosity. There were no hidden agendas, no ulterior motives—just a desire to learn more about one another. Talking did not involve venting about dissatisfaction, expressing negative feelings about the relationship, interrogations, or attempts to change each other. Instead, it was about the joy of mutual revelation. As a relationship matures, this same spirit of openness, curiosity, and nonjudgment facilitates more intimacy.

Remember that every person communicates differently. Some might articulate their thoughts quickly with lots of words, while others may require more time and use few words. A person who prefers fewer words isn't necessarily less engaged, just as someone who uses many words isn't necessarily better at expressing themselves. Some people speak in an animated way with their hands while others remain quite still. Communication styles vary greatly and fostering intimacy requires patience and the willingness to make room for whatever form of expression emerges.

It's good to remember that dialogue isn't the same as monologue, and listening doesn't mean *not* talking. Balance between speakers is important, even if that means making room for silence. Many people who use a lot of words are unaware of how much they monopolize the conversation and control what gets talked about, even when the other person is trying to say something. It might be useful to give each person a time limit at first, say, five minutes, during which they talk and the partner doesn't. Once the partner has reflected back what was heard and understood, they can switch roles. It sounds technical, but it might help to make sure each partner gets the air time they need to express themselves, especially when you're just getting started with the practice.

Interrupting can also be useful when it is for the sake of reflecting back what has been said so the speaker feels heard (*not* for changing the subject abruptly or countering what is being said with your own perspective). It's okay to slow things down if your partner is jumping from subject to subject and example to example. Jump in, but for the sake of reflecting back what you heard and understood up to that point.

* * *

When we first got together, I always had to hold Matthew's hand or be sitting close beside him. I admit it! I was "needy" of touch and attention. I'd have my hand on his leg or tickling his neck when we were driving. I initiated most of the touch, and the more, the better, as far as I was concerned. He didn't seem to mind either—which was great!

One day, early on in our married life together, Matthew and I were in the main living area of our home. Matthew was on the couch on his laptop, and I was pretending to be busy doing something at the dining room table.

That day, I had decided I was going to wait for him to initiate affectionate contact with me. I waited…and waited…and waited some more…silently hoping he would mosey on over to me, wrap his beautiful arms around me, and hold me tight for a bit. This did not happen.

In fact, nothing happened. I glanced sideways at him many times only to see the same picture: Matthew engrossed in what he was doing. I was not on his radar. I was not a thought in his mind—or at least, that is the story I was telling myself. In fact, it felt as though I could cease to exist altogether, and he wouldn't even notice!

Big feelings were brewing inside of me, until, finally, I couldn't contain my emotional distress any longer and burst out with a head-on attack: "You aren't *ever* going to approach me, are you?! It doesn't matter to you if I'm here or not!"

Matthew was startled, to say the least, and quickly jumped to his own defense: "I'm on my computer! What's your problem?!"

I moved in closer, turning up the volume on my emotions, laying into him about the lack of attention he was paying me. My tears were soon flowing and Matthew was on high alert, looking for the nearest exit. This was our attack-defend cycle in our earlier days, triggering raw spots (echoes from the past) for both of us.

At that point, I had yet to learn how to ask for what I wanted or needed in a non-demanding way. I was still getting to know my own shadow parts and learning to incorporate and integrate them into myself and our relationship. This is where "just talking" has helped us so much.

I have gotten to know myself better through our conversations as well as how I impact Matthew's raw spots when I attack him. He's come to appreciate my sensitivities and see through my big emotions to the real need underneath: his loving attention. In fact, I'm a lot more secure now and much less "needy" as we have developed much more reliable, authentic intimacy over the years.

* * *

Choose a location where both of you feel at ease and safe, away from any potential interruptions. Set the intention of actively listening, understanding, and keeping an open mind. Approach the conversation with a willingness to explore, learn, and grow. Ensure you are physically comfortable and emotionally calm before starting the discussion. This might mean having a soothing cup of tea, taking a few deep breaths, or doing a quick mindfulness exercise (easily found on google) to center and ground yourselves.

As you prepare yourselves for a meaningful conversation (maybe a half an hour long) about intimacy, each of you are invited to choose two words from the following list that feel relevant to you personally…

1. Trust

2. Communication

3. Vulnerability

4. Understanding

5. Affection

6. Compassion

7. Honesty

8. Empathy

9. Bonding

10. Closeness

11. Tenderness

12. Passion

13. Connection

14. Eroticism

15. Sharing

16. Touch

17. Emotional openness

18. Safety

19. Mutual respect

20. Deep understanding

Should you think of a word related to intimacy that holds significance to you and isn't listed here, please feel free to incorporate it into your discussion. Reflect on your chosen words, what they mean to you, and how you would like them to manifest more in your relationship. Focus on the present and the future as much as possible (rather than complaining about the past), depicting your desires. Frame your thoughts positively, focusing on what you *do* desire and value rather than what you don't. Speak about yourself rather than your partner to minimize blame, accusations, and criticism. This conversation is not about judging right or wrong, demanding, or reaching an agreement. It's about trying to understand your partner's unique perspective on intimacy by *just talking*.

The second key practice for attaining intimacy in a relationship is to *touch*. Humans are wired for touch. Touch is one of the fundamental modes of sensory perception and plays a crucial role in human development, communication, and emotional well-being. From infancy, touch is vital. Skin-to-skin contact between a newborn and its mother or primary caregiver facilitates bonding and has been shown to offer several health benefits for the baby, including stabilization of heart rate, improved oxygen saturation rates, and pain relief. Research has demonstrated that infants who are deprived of touch, such as those in orphanages with minimal physical contact, can experience developmental delays, emotional disturbances, and failure to thrive, meaning they die.

Human skin contains a myriad of endings that transmit tactile information to the brain. Specialized nerve fibers known as C-tactile afferents are designed specifically to detect gentle, stroking touch and are believed to be linked to emotional responses. Touch also activates the brain's orbitofrontal cortex, which is linked to feelings, indicating the profound connection between touch and emotion. Physical touch can stimulate the release of oxytocin, often referred to as the "love hormone." This neurochemical plays a role in social bonding and fosters feelings of connectedness and trust. Studies have shown that massage and therapeutic touch can reduce cortisol (stress hormone) levels and increase feelings of well-being.

Physical touch, such as hugs or massages, has been associated with reduced blood pressure, lower heart rate, and increased immune function. Simple gestures like a pat on the back or holding hands can convey a myriad of emotions, from comfort and compassion, to reassurance, often more powerfully than words. Many adults are starved for touch.

Noted psychologist, sex therapist, and researcher Barry McCarthy emphasizes the importance of touch in couple relationships in his book *Rekindling Desire* (2014). According to McCarthy, there are different forms of touch, each with its own significance: affectionate, sensual, playful, sexual, and erotic. While some touch can be flirtatious and sexually suggestive, like a playful smack or grab, touch can also be tender and comforting, devoid of sexual undertones. Like we can *just talk*, touch can be *just touch*. We need to get back to the basics and remember that skin-to-skin touch is pleasurable and a basic need in and of itself.

Research suggests that even small gestures involving touch can be incredibly impactful. A six-second kiss, for instance, can create a profound sense of connection and affection (Gottman & Silver, 1999). Similarly, a long, heartfelt hug can communicate more than a thousand words. In this way, touch becomes a silent language, a vital tool for maintaining and nurturing intimacy.

It is also important to acknowledge and respect that not everyone is innately touchy-feely and some people feel trapped or suffocated when holding hands or cuddling. Each individual's comfort with and desire for touch is influenced by a range of factors, including their upbringing, past experiences, personality type, and even their current mood or state of health. For those who are less comfortable with touch, the journey toward incorporating more physical intimacy into their relationships may be slower, and that's perfectly okay.

Consider creating a "menu" of touch in your relationship. This could include anything from holding hands and cuddling to giving each other massages or simply resting your head on your partner's shoulder. These interactions should not necessarily lead to sexual activity, but can instead serve to create a stronger sense of closeness and physical intimacy. Notice the contrast in how you're willing to give touch and how you wish to receive touch, as these can be significantly different. Keep in mind that everyone has unique preferences when it comes to touch, including the type, timing, and place.

Brainstorm the kinds of touch you each enjoy or desire and the related *who, what, when, where, why,* and *how* components. This could be anything from a gentle hand squeeze to a full-body massage, from a lingering kiss to playful tickling. Be sure to discuss the specific areas where you like to be touched, the times and places when you would welcome touch, and the kinds of touch that make you feel most loved and connected. Remember, the aim here is to focus on what you *do* like. Frame your desires positively.

Once you have created your customized "touch menu," choose one type of touch each week to consciously practice giving to your partner. Make a deliberate effort to incorporate this touch into your daily interactions as one way to "feed the pet" as discussed in Chapter Seven. The type of touch does not always have to be complex or time-consuming. It could be as simple as giving your partner a hug before you leave for work or a kiss goodnight. The key here is consistency. Make it a routine part of your shared life.

The third key practice to enhance intimacy in a relationship is to *pleasure* each other. Pleasure is not often used as a verb in this way but it follows suit with the other practices for attaining the principle of intimacy: talk, touch, and pleasure. Dr. Peggy Kleinplatz embarked on a research project with the question, "What type of sex would be worth having?" Her findings showed that the most satisfying sexual experiences are those that prioritize pleasure, connection, and mutual exploration over specific acts or outcomes (Kleinplatz & Menard, 2020).

Often, couples tend to focus on intercourse and orgasm, which can inadvertently transform their sexual encounters into goal-oriented, performance-based, anxiety-provoking tasks—like a challenging chore. This approach can detract from the overall experience, reducing the pleasure and connection that can be derived from intimacy. By shifting focus from goals like intercourse and orgasm to pleasure, couples can become more immersed in the moment and explore a wider spectrum of sensual experiences.

In her book *Come As You Are* (2015), sex educator and author Dr. Emily Nagoski introduces the concept of the "dual control model." This model, akin to a car's accelerator and brake system, involves elements that enhance and inhibit sexual responsiveness. "Accelerators" are things that drive us toward sexual pleasure; turn-ons could include physical attraction, romantic emotions, certain smells or sounds, or explicit sexual cues like flirtation. On the other hand, "brakes" are things that inhibit sexual responsiveness. These turn-offs could include stress, fear, lack of trust, negative body image, or past traumas. Lots of people are aware of what turns them on but don't give much thought to the idea of turn-offs. It's important to be aware of both turn-ons and turn-offs for each partner and to take them into consideration when planning to connect.

Incorporating a "connection date"—rather than a typical date night—into your routine can significantly deepen the intimacy in your relationship. Partners can take turns planning scenarios specifically geared toward physical (and emotional) connection. Make eating an intimate activity by feeding one another dinner or dessert. To make it more sensual, choose certain foods like chocolate-covered strawberries or cheese and grapes if you don't have a sweet tooth.

One partner might organize a candlelit massage, while the other could arrange a party for two of slow dancing at home. Plan a sexy scenario that turns the "on's" on and the "offs" off as per Emily Nagoski's model. These dates should focus on activities that are mutually pleasurable.

Strive to make your intimate encounters about enjoyment and pleasure rather than achieving a specific goal. Explore each other's bodies without an agenda, communicate about what feels good, and be present and engaged in the moment. Don't focus solely on erogenous zones, especially when getting started. Guide your partner's hand to communicate if words are too awkward. Limit the time for pleasurable touch as desired ahead of time. In essence, prioritizing pleasure over performance, emphasizing connection over completion, and focusing on intimacy rather than intercourse can elevate your shared experience and enhance the passion in your relationship.

* * *

Simone and Frank settle into their living room, a sense of purpose uniting them as they planned to talk about intimacy using the three practices.

Simone (jumping right in): "So, we both want to spice things up, huh? What's on your mind?"

Frank (with a hesitant but hopeful tone): "Well, you know I'm more visual. I'd love to see you more…more of you…maybe we could try lighting a candle?"

Simone (a bit self-conscious but intrigued): "A candle could work. I'm not ready for full lights, but I can do a candle."

Frank (smiling): "And maybe you could wear something…sexy? Some lingerie?"

Simone (laughing, her mood lightening): "It's been ages, but why not? I'd like to mix it up too. Maybe we start outside the bedroom? How about this: I put the kids to bed, come downstairs, and find a surprise waiting for me in the living room? There are a couple candles and you're standing there…with that look in your eyes."

Frank (playful): "Yeah, 'Hey, do you come here often?'"

They both laugh, easing the tension.

Simone (saying what she does want): "But let's keep it light, no expectations. That's a turn-off for me. And make sure the blinds are closed!"

Frank (nodding): "Yeah, we don't want an audience. We'll take it slow, see where it goes…no pressure."

Their conversation is filled with excited glances and giggles. They're taking baby steps, openly sharing their desires, and gradually understanding each other's "accelerators" and "brakes." This gentle, open dialogue is their first step toward a deeper, more intimate connection. Frank and Simone are happy just to be talking about it, finally!

Exercise: Let's Talk About Touch

For this exercise, it's essential to start by understanding what affectionate touch is. Affectionate touch is gentle, respectful, and nonsexual. It's the hand on your partner's back (not breast or butt!) while cooking together, the intertwining of fingers while walking, or a soft kiss on the forehead. It's about expressing love, care, and closeness without sexual undertones. It is not groping or any style of touch that feels intrusive, awkward, or uncomfortable.

In this exercise, start a conversation with your partner about touch. Discuss whether it's easier for you to give affectionate touch or receive it and explore why. It's perfectly fine if you're not naturally "touchy-feely" and it's equally okay if you love both: being touched and touching. Everyone has unique preferences, and whatever your comfort level is, it's normal. You're not competing with your partner or comparing your comfort level to anyone else's.

During this conversation, delve into potential vulnerabilities linked with touch. Are there fears of rejection or feelings of unworthiness? Do you feel like you're lowering yourself if you initiate affection? Does feeling pleasure through touch make you feel uncomfortable? Is there any other emotional issue associated with touch? Open up to your partner about these feelings.

This exercise is designed to be short, straightforward, and non-judgmental. It's a tool to foster understanding, openness, and respect for each other's comfort and preferences around touch, in order to enhance your connection and intimacy.

12

Community

"Remember, we're all in this alone."
– Lily Tomlin

I was 22 and a single mother. I didn't have a completed education, a job, or any source of income. I didn't have close friends or family around me. I ended up getting welfare and was thankful that the government paid for a crib for my son to sleep in. I didn't have a car or a home. I felt lost and alone in a world I knew next-to-nothing about with a newborn infant strapped on my back.

After moving back in with my parents, I found myself, once again, in the country, isolated and dependent. I drove from Onondaga to McMaster University in Hamilton that winter, taking night courses on a "letter of permission" from the University of Toronto. Typically given only under exceptional circumstances, the letter allowed me to take courses at another university while still technically graduating from U of T.

It was at this time that I joined the women's group even though I hadn't ever thought of myself as abused. It was new to sit, hip-to-hip, in a circle of women on a motley assortment of old chairs and couches. I liked feeling *squeezed* between them the first night when there were almost more bodies than seats.

I loved doing "round robins" and "check-ins." Every woman got a chance to share and be heard. It was new to have so much attention all at once when it was my turn to share. It was great to be together with the goal of getting to know each other. Bev talked about her husband's betrayal. Jill vented about her parents and how they interfered with the way she wanted to raise her teenage daughter. Christine often laughed as she talked about her seven children—the eighth on the way—while the rest of us sat with wide eyes, our mouths hanging open, wondering how she managed all the chaos. No one was overlooked or forgotten. Sure, each woman had the option to pass, but no one was ignored.

The counselor kept things flowing naturally. She made us feel safe and skillfully led us in conversations about our lives and perspectives on relationships, asking questions and making comments, linking the similarities between us, and encouraging us to think for ourselves. It felt like she was part of the group—an equal not an authority figure.

A core group of about eight of us formed over the weeks and months as we progressed through the three stages of the program. We were different in so many ways—in terms of age, race, socioeconomic status, and education—but we had all been abused and/or neglected by our partners (and often others too). We were all at different places regarding our healing journeys, but we had one thing in common: We wanted to be happier and have healthier romantic relationships.

It didn't take long before these women became like sisters. I would think about them, look forward to our next gathering, and have questions to ask them or things I couldn't wait to tell them. We cried, laughed, and were outraged—and then somber—as we reflected together on new ideas and the state of our lives. There was a warmth between us that reached well beyond what I had expected from a publicly funded support group.

My outlook and approach to life was transformed by my experience in this women's group. I learned about parenting and healthy relationships and was even encouraged to do a Master of Social Work degree. I got in touch with myself *on the inside*, a place I had never really known was there—my roots. I became familiar with my likes and dislikes. I became better at identifying and expressing my feelings. I gained a sense of self-worth I hadn't known before.

After getting my MSW degree, I found the courage I needed to work as a counselor myself and pushed through all the times I had impostor syndrome (feeling like a fraud or fake), felt not good enough, and doubted my abilities. My self-confidence has continued to grow since then, as I have kept taking personal and professional risks, believing good things *can* happen.

I was able to filter out the kind of men that weren't a healthy choice for me when I started online dating and ultimately found Matthew to share my life with, having a much greater sense of who I was, what I wanted, and what I would not tolerate.

I will be forever grateful for my beloved counselor and "family of friends" as I used to call our women's group. I would never have been able to achieve any of these things without their support. Although I didn't realize it at the time, what I experienced in that group was the transformative power of community.

* * *

The principles we've explored so far have implied a kind of bubble (or chrysalis!) around you and your partner, as a couple. But the truth is that couples exist within a much larger interdependent ecosystem that includes all of humanity. Couples need the last principle of the Butterfly Blueprint—authentic *community*—in order to grow and evolve. Interdependence works both ways, *within* couples and *between* couples. Just like any ecosystem found in nature, whether micro or macro, all life is connected internally and externally ad infinitum, in both the world of roots and the world of branches.

The migration of monarch butterflies presents a vivid metaphor for an interdependent community. Monarchs, known for their striking orange and black wings, undertake an incredible journey, spanning thousands of miles all the way from Canada to Mexico, making them one of the world's most famous long-distance insect migrants.

Remarkably, this migration occurs over several generations of butterflies. The individual monarch that begins the journey will not be the one that completes it. Instead, it's the collective effort of multiple generations, each completing a leg of the journey, that ensures the survival of the species. Just as the monarch migration relies on the interconnectedness and cooperation of multiple generations, so, too, does an interdependent human community rely on the participation and contribution of all its members over time.

Moreover, throughout their migration and life cycle, monarchs depend on a specific plant: milkweed. Monarch caterpillars feed exclusively on the leaves of milkweed plants. Without milkweed, they cannot complete their life cycle and migration. This dependence highlights how each part of an ecosystem relies on other parts and how changes to one part have a significant impact on the whole.

Monarchs also cluster together in vast numbers during their winter hibernation. This behavior demonstrates how, even in the animal kingdom, there's safety and strength in community. These clusters not only provide necessary warmth but also help protect the butterflies from predators.

Community is essential to humanity's evolution; we need to be emotionally *in touch* with other couples. Scott M. Peck, an American psychiatrist and author of *The Road Less Traveled* (1978), defines community as "a group of two or more people who, regardless of the diversity of their backgrounds, have been able to accept and transcend their differences, enabling them to communicate openly and effectively and to work together toward common goals, while having a sense of unusual safety with one another." As we have seen throughout this book, a "group of two" can be two partners in a couple providing an environment or community for one another. Likewise, two or more couples can make a community—a group of pairs who face similar challenges and share the goal of wanting to achieve healthy interdependence in their relationships.

We all live in a community: a village, city, or town. There's some kind of neighborhood or local culture. But most of us never actually *experience* community. When you *experience* community, you know what it's like to feel seen for who you really are and supported in becoming your very best. You don't feel shame since you are loved and accepted as you are, like that "as is" Ikea furniture. In authentic community, you're an integral piece of the puzzle, irreplaceable in the hearts and minds of the others, and they each have a special place in your heart and mind too.

Many of us don't have a lot of positive examples of what being in a couple can look and feel like. Mostly, we learn from our parents—or sometimes our grandparents—and often, these examples were more about what *not* to do. Culturally, the focus is on individuality and independence at the expense of couple connection. Personal goals are promoted and success is measured by educational and professional achievements, resulting in work-life imbalance. Materialism and consumerism lead couples to prioritize external accomplishments over the emotional depth of their partnership. Shifting gender roles present a further challenge to traditional relationship models.

In our interconnected and digital age, couples often find themselves in the grips of comparison and competition via social media, whether consciously or unconsciously. The portrayals of "perfect relationships" on Facebook, in movies, or even among peer groups can inadvertently set unrealistic standards. This leads to couples feeling pressured to measure up or present an idealized version of their relationship, obscuring the truth.

The sitcom *Friends* is celebrated for its portrayal of a close-knit group or community of six friends and their journey through the ups and downs of adulthood in New York City. Each character had distinct "flaws"—Ross's insecurity, Rachel's materialism, Monica's compulsiveness, Chandler's sarcasm, Joey's simplicity, and Phoebe's eccentricity. Yet, these traits were accepted and often lovingly teased by the group, demonstrating a deep understanding of each other's humanity. Each one belonged and felt safe in their community of friends.

Although Matthew and I have never been part of an ongoing couples' community, we did attend a "Hold Me Tight" couples retreat in Costa Rica. These retreats are based on Sue Johnson's work in emotionally focused therapy. I've also helped to facilitate Hold Me Tight couples' retreats. These brief but powerful opportunities to participate in group work for couples reinforced my belief that it's a necessary part of the journey of interdependence.

Seeing other couples navigate the ebbs and flows of their relationships normalizes the challenges all couples face, decreasing shame and the urge to hide during tough times. A couples' community reinforces the idea that love is an ongoing commitment that requires repeated, conscious efforts. It provides tangible examples of how to maintain and strengthen a marital bond. Observational learning and shared experiences offer valuable lessons and inspiration, as couples celebrate their wins and support one another through their sorrows. Just as individual growth toward wholeness is nurtured by the "mirror" one's partner provides, a couple's evolution can be bolstered by the collective wisdom and support of other couples within a community.

In this sense, interdependence is a concept that applies to the microcosm of a couple's relationship *and* the macrocosm of a community of couples. In fact, one could extend this further and say that countries would also benefit from taking on an interdependent approach to international relations. Planet Earth is an ecosystem that requires humanity to live as one big, interdependent family. The following three Venn diagrams show how the Butterfly Blueprint principles and practices can be applied to our whole world since everything and everyone in this world is made up of two sides and a coin!

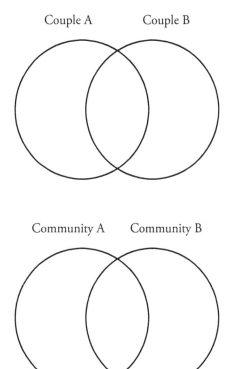

Country A   Country B

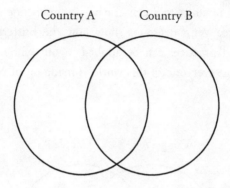

In a society with ample support groups for various challenges, couples often find themselves underserved. If you're grappling with addiction, eating disorders, or mental health issues, there's no shortage of groups to turn to. For those undergoing the pain of grief or parenting issues, there are dedicated spaces offering solace and understanding. Yet when it comes to couples—the most foundational relationship for all of society—resources seem scarce.

This is surprising, especially when we consider the integral role romantic partnership plays in most people's lives. Dr. Sue Johnson likes to say, "These days, most of us live in a community of two," meaning a person and their partner. Many couples move around to different cities for work and have family scattered all over the province, country, or globe!

While society provides support for many of life's challenges, it seems that couples, at least for now, are somewhat on their own. It's high time we recognize the unique challenges couples face and work toward creating supportive couples' communities. Someone has to take the initiative to get things started, though. Maybe that someone is you!

A couples' community could grow out of a church group, where people come together not only for spiritual growth but also to build stronger interdependent relationships. Or think about organizing a group of couples with a local counselor as your facilitator, where partners can share their journeys—the ups and downs—and learn from each other. For those who prefer the digital world, consider organizing an online forum or social media group, a place where couples from various locations can virtually meet, share, and support one another. Thanks to COVID-19, everyone is comfortable with Zoom, and it's easy to turn your laptop into a portal for couple community. You could even start a group in your neighborhood, with a mention in the local newspaper to attract other interested couples to join. The idea is to create spaces where couples can connect, support, and grow together. You can also join our growing community and interactive program for couples online at www.butterflyblueprint-book.com! This group focuses on the present and future rather than bringing up the past unnecessarily. It's psycho-educational and also provides opportunities to learn from and interact with other couples.

Just as with all the other principles in the Butterfly Blueprint, a duality often hinders couples from engaging in authentic community with other couples: the *public-private* dilemma in which one partner is more transparent and likes to talk with others about their relationship, while the other partner is more reserved. Perhaps, both partners are ambivalent and have mixed feelings about "going public." While it might be a relief to open up in some ways, it could be embarrassing in others.

This conundrum is captured by Lily Tomlin's famous quote written at the beginning of this chapter: "We're all in this alone." While we live as couples in the public domain, we usually suffer our relationship struggles in painful isolation. The public-private duality dilemma makes it hard to find the support and encouragement we need to succeed on the path toward effective interdependence.

At the heart of this tension is a deeply ingrained belief that couple challenges are meant to be solved behind closed doors. This perspective is reinforced by cultural stigmas that make admitting relationship difficulties feel like airing dirty laundry. Many are afraid if they open up—even to family—that other people's opinions of their partners will change (which can happen), leading to awkward, divided loyalties at future gatherings. Many believe they should be able to manage their relationship issues independently and that it's a sign of weakness to need help.

But the truth is a couple's journey isn't isolated. Every couple, no matter how unique, navigates universal challenges. When couples get trapped between the fear of publicly admitting they have issues and the longing to be more genuinely connected with other couples, they unknowingly cut themselves off from the possibility of experiencing true community. By stepping beyond the public-private duality dilemma and engaging with the principle of community directly, couples find a clearer path to interdependence, leaning on and learning from others on a similar journey.

In the beginning of my career, I was hired as the "Violence Against Women" counselor at a local family counseling agency. I worked mainly with abused women and built a group program there like the one I had been through myself. Oftentimes, the women shied away from the idea of joining the group. I had to sell it to a lot of women. The funny thing is, when the time came for the group to end, many of them wanted to find a way to keep it going—even on their own.

At times in life, what we need might not align with what we want. Like taking bitter medicine, despite the resistance, it's the remedy that brings healing and relief. A community for couples may appear challenging or intimidating at first. The thought of exposing and admitting relationship challenges might seem unpalatable but the benefits of such a community are immeasurable.

The benefit of community is mirrored in other groups, like those related to addiction recovery. Consider Alcoholics Anonymous (AA), an organization that's helped countless individuals overcome their addictions through community support. While the nature of addiction and relationship challenges differ, there are intriguing parallels. In relationships, we might find ourselves habitually leaning into roles or patterns—like always needing to be right, indulging in constant complaining, or perpetually playing the victim. These behaviors, much like addiction, can become deeply ingrained and hard to break away from without the right support. It's worth noting that while AA doesn't provide a magic formula, it does offer an environment where individuals can find support and tools to combat their addiction, *together*.

As Aristotle said, "What society honors will be cultivated." Couples, in the right community setting, can find the strength to break free from the unhealthy cycles that trap them. They can discover new perspectives, share insights, and even lean on other couples during tough times. The leap to participate might feel risky, but for many, the experience is the medicine their relationship needs, just what the doctor ordered!

When you contemplate the possibility of experiencing community in a group of couples, a lot of options open up. You might decide to become a part of a community that's already established. Or perhaps you'll feel inspired to pave your own path, starting something that's uniquely yours. You might want to start off with just one other couple, or you might feel more comfortable in a group of many other couples, so it feels less intense. The structure could be formal or laidback. Regardless of these details, there are three foundational practices that should be at the heart of any community you consider.

The first key practice in attaining the principle of community is showing *respect*. Couples in the community shouldn't intrude on other couples' bubbles, just as partners shouldn't criticize, complain, or attack one another. They should refrain from expressing opinions, giving unsolicited advice, making assumptions, or jumping to conclusions about other couples—especially those based on biases, stereotypes, or superficial observations. Showing respect in this space means giving each couple the room to express their unique perspectives and experiences without an immediate rush to judge, label, "fix," or critique.

Begin by adopting a foundational perspective: Assume everyone in the community is the way they are for very good reasons, rooted in past experience, *just like you*. Every emotional reaction and strongly held belief often makes complete sense when viewed through the lens of a person's life story and past relationships.

Reflect on the tree analogy, understanding that while we see the branches of someone's behavior and choices, there's an entire unseen world of roots beneath, rich with complex stories. When someone's actions or words seem puzzling or aversive, give them the benefit of the doubt. Foster a mindset of listening and curiosity. Ask yourself, "What might I be missing in my perception of other couples in this community?" and "How can I exercise the principles and practices of the Butterfly Blueprint now, with these other couples?"

Be acutely aware of the personal, subjective lens through which you view others. Remember, we see branches not roots. Our perceptions are filtered by our own experiences, beliefs, histories, and emotions. We tell ourselves stories, but more often than not, these narratives capture only a fraction of the truth. Embrace humility and recognize you don't see things objectively; you don't see the big picture, how things truly are. Accept that we all harbor stereotypes and biases. It's a part of being human. But we can choose not to be defined or limited by them. Challenge your immediate assumptions—the hasty categories you form or the labels you assign. Instead of leaning into these, push them aside. Familiarize yourself with your own biases. Writing them down can be helpful. Regularly revisit this list, refining and expanding it as your self-awareness grows.

Differences are inevitable. Each couple, with their distinct backgrounds and stories, brings a world of differing viewpoints to the community. These differences need to be embraced rather than dismissed. This means appreciating that multiple perspectives and approaches can coexist harmoniously, even when they seem to oppose each other, when we acknowledge, accept, and accommodate one another's differences (the fourth principle of the blueprint).

Risk is the second key practice in attaining the principle of community as a couple. Building deeper connections, fostering understanding, and promoting growth within a couples' community require individuals and couples to take risks. Stepping out of our comfort zones and pushing beyond the boundaries of what is familiar can be daunting, yet it is in this unfamiliar terrain that true growth occurs. Venturing into uncharted territory can feel like speaking a foreign language and struggling to find the right words. But taking risks forges new paths and creates the potential for lasting bonds to form within a couples' community.

When couples risk sharing parts of their stories, they open up a window into their lives and expose their innermost selves, allowing others to better understand their struggles, joys, and lessons learned. This openness is what makes genuine connections and mutual understanding possible. Similarly, actively listening to others can be a risk, especially if a perspective is different from your own. Truly hearing what another person or couple is sharing can be transformative, fostering deeper empathy and connection.

Brené Brown's work emphasizes that avoiding the risk of openness in relationships can lead to a loss of love, belonging, and joy—the very elements of wholehearted living. Taking the leap to share experiences, struggles, and triumphs with other couples—getting in the ring—can be a profound act of courage. It is through these authentic exchanges that deeper connections are formed (Brown, 2010).

As you navigate the couples' community, you will come across new perspectives and insights. But by voicing a unique perspective, you contribute to the discussion and broaden the ideas shared within the community. More often than not, another participant will agree (even if in secret) and feel relieved that someone spoke up. Taking the risk to share often gives others the "permission" to do the same.

In the pursuit of becoming a more interdependent couple by fostering community, the third practice is to *rejoice*. It's a gift to find other couples willing to engage in community, sharing the goal of evolving from the sweetness of chocolate love to a conscious and purposeful, interdependent, whole, and intimate form of love. Such a journey, like the symbol of a koru—an unfurling fern frond—brings new life, growth, strength, and peace to our relationships and provides the contrasts we need to truly feel alive. Authentic community is worth celebrating!

We can rejoice in the knowledge we gain. We are limited by our perceptions, and this is why we depend on others to catch a glimpse of the bigger picture, assembling all the pieces of the puzzle together. Through shared experiences, we learn *not* to trust the stories we tell ourselves, and come to understand the power of unity in their place.

We can rejoice in sharing our journeys, exploring the ups and downs of trying to implement the eight principles and 24 practices of becoming an interdependent couple together. Our combined efforts to embrace the principles of surrender, equality, generosity, differentiation, unity, wholeness, intimacy, and community lead us to a shared destination: effective interdependence. Together, we learn how to be complementary instead of conflictual, how to construct rather than destroy, and build rather than break.

The Butterfly Blueprint serves as a compass or North Star on this journey, revealing the ever-present, though sometimes hidden, wholeness that is always before us. The Blueprint lights the way toward greater alignment with the butterfly metaphor, transcending our individual limitations and expanding beyond our own set of wings. It's essential to remember no person will ever be perfect, nor will any couple. What truly matters is the choice to work and grow together, as individuals, as couples, and as communities of couples. That choice is worthy of celebration!

Becoming an interdependent couple is not just about reaching a destination but embracing the process itself. It's about acknowledging the struggles and celebrating the victories, no matter how small. It is about finding the joy in the act of coming together, gathering, like a murmuration of birds gracefully flying through the sky. In rejoicing, we fuel the spark of community, encouraging others to join the process of growth and connection as interdependent couples. We both build the community around us and benefit from it at the same time, just as we do within our own couple.

We can celebrate the fact that we have a book to help us, a blueprint to follow, and companions to walk alongside us. *The Butterfly Blueprint* is a gift that not only shows us the way but highlights the beauty of the work itself. Like the "butterfly effect," it's a reminder of our interconnectedness, illustrating how even the smallest of actions—a single flutter—can have significant impacts across the globe. It inspires us to build a strong, loving community of couples, where every small step, every gentle flutter, contributes to a larger, transformative wave of change and interdependent connection, transforming life and the whole world for all humanity.

CONCLUSION

"You have escaped the cage. Your wings are spread out. Now fly."
– Rumi

*Y*ou *can* both win. You just have to decide that that's *truly* what you want: to *both* win. The Butterfly Blueprint principles and practices teach you how to give and get the love you want by loving the "third body" that connects and includes both of you: the butterfly.

As Susan Cain writes in her book *Bittersweet* (2022), longing is the creative force that moves us toward belonging. We attain healthy interdependence when we yearn for love. We reach divine communion when "I am for my beloved and my beloved is for me" (Song of Solomon 6:3).

While one set of wings is more masculine and the other set more feminine, a battle of the sexes doesn't have to dominate and destroy the relationship. Instead, they can evolve together, blending their unique strengths and further developing their weaknesses, to embrace and celebrate their shared humanity.

Mother Nature is the villain and the hero of the human story! She set us up in two worlds, the external world of branches and the internal world of roots, so we would see how we depend on one another to become whole, intimate, and fulfilled with an abundance we never imagined possible.

We are interdependent whether we like it or not. We need one another whether we like it or not. When the honeymoon ends and Mother Nature pulls the switch in the bait-and-switch manoeuvre, don't doubt or despair. Don't trust the stories you tell yourself. The switch is an opportunity—a new beginning for you and your partner to use your relationship like a mini laboratory. You can practice together and evolve into your best selves *through* your relationship.

You can get into the *driver's* seat and transcend the "what's in it *for me,*" self-absorbed approach of chocolate love. You can expand your perception of reality by considering the connection between you and your partner, the empty space between you that becomes an abundant shared place when you ask, "What's in it *for us?*" You can create compatibility consciously!

The Butterfly Blueprint is a transformative tool for couples facing common challenges related to money, sex, parenting, running a household, in-laws, and addictions. This approach transforms potential conflicts into collaborative discussions by acknowledging one another's perspectives and aiming for middle ground. Each partner seeks understanding rather than victory over the other.

A caterpillar doesn't exactly die. It transforms into a butterfly. Life and death are intertwined in a cyclical process of renewal and rebirth. Transformation is the middle line between life and death that acknowledges their interconnectedness and the potential for growth, change, and continuation in different forms.

Imaginal cells exist in the caterpillar but are dormant. They become active during the pupa stage, directing the development of the adult butterfly's features (like wings and legs). Just as the dormant imaginal cells in a caterpillar hold the promise of transformation, couples can harness their imagination and creativity to foster growth and bring about positive changes in their relationship, unlocking potential they might not have realized was there.

The chaos and confusion inside a chrysalis end with the birth of a beautiful butterfly! Just as the butterfly must struggle to emerge from its chrysalis, pushing fluid into its wings to strengthen them for flight, your struggles can transform into a new beginning for your relationship too, if you—yourself—take radical responsibility and proactively aim your efforts and your imagination toward connection.

Remember, there aren't any bad guys, so put away your detective hats. The duality dilemmas are there because opposites attract *and* repel; both of you are irreplaceable just like a butterfly needs two equal and opposite sets of wings to fly. The key is learning how to harmonize and complement one another, finding the middle ground based on cooperation rather than domination and conflict.

The benefits are endless, for your kids, your extended family, neighbors, and friends. Couples, communities, and even countries can consciously connect interdependently with the same approach! By engaging in this work, you're contributing to world peace and becoming an example for the rest of humanity.

Lead the way in your couple! Teach your partner how to do it! Start your own group or sign up for our growing online couples' community at butterflyblueprintbook.com. It's the perfect place to share, grow, and connect so we can keep all our hearts fluttering forever, as one big, beautiful butterfly!

THE BUTTERFLY
BLUEPRINT SUMMARY

Principles, Dualities, and Practices

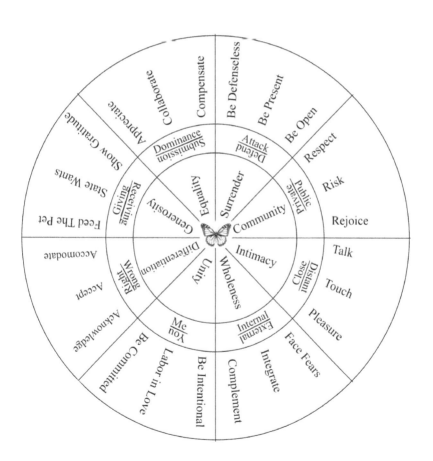

REFERENCES

Adams, J.S. (1963). Towards an understanding of inequity. *The journal of abnormal and social psychology,* Volume 67, No. 5.

Beattie, M. (2022). *Codependent no more: How to stop controlling others and start caring for yourself.* Harper/Hazelden.

Becker, G. (1997). *The gift of fear: Survival signals that protect us from violence.* Dell Publishing.

Blake, W. (1994). *The marriage of heaven and hell.* Dover Publications.

Bly, R. (1999). *Eating the honey of words: New and selected poems.* Harper.

Bowen, M. (1993). *Family therapy in clinical practice.* Jason Aronson, Inc.

Branden, N. (1988). *How to raise your self-esteem: The proven action-oriented approach to greater self-respect and self-confidence.* Bantam.

Branden, N. (1995). *The six pillars of self-esteem: The definitive work on self-esteem by the leading pioneer in the field.* Bantam.

Brown, B. (2010). *The gifts of imperfection: Let go of who you think you're supposed to be and embrace who you are.* Hazelden.

Brown, B. (2012). *Daring greatly: How the courage to be vulnerable transforms the way we live, love, parent, and lead.* Gotham Books.

Cain, S. (2022). *Bittersweet: How sorrow and longing make us whole.* Crown.

Cameron, J. (2002). *The artist's way: A spiritual path to higher creativity.* Tarcher/Putnam

Chapman, G. (2010). *The five love languages.* Northfield Publishing.

Clear, J. (2018). *Atomic habits: An easy and proven way to build good habits and break bad ones.* Avery.

Eisenberger, N. I., Lieberman, M. D., & Williams, K. D. (2003). Does rejection hurt? An fMRI study of social exclusion. *Science, 302*(5643), 290–292.

Gibran, K. (2003). *The prophet.* Rupa & Co.

Glover, R. A. (2000). *No more Mr. Nice Guy.* Running Press.

Gottman, J. & DeClaire, J. (2002). *The relationship cure: A 5 step guide to strengthening your marriage, family, and friendships.* Harmony/Rodale.

Gottman, J., Gottman, J. S., Abrams, D., & Carlton Abrams, R. (2018). *Eight dates: Essential conversations for a lifetime of love.* Workman Publishing Co., Inc.

Gottman, J., Gottman, J. S., & DeClaire, J. (2006). *Ten lessons to transform your marriage: America's Love Lab experts share their strategies for strengthening your relationship.* Three Rivers Press.

Gottman, J. & Silver, N. (1999). *The seven principles for making marriage work: A practical guide from the country's foremost relationship expert.* Crown Publishers.

Hendrix, H. (1988). *Getting the love you want: A guide for couples.* St. Martin's Griffin.

Howes, L. (2021, August 10). *The biggest reasons 80% of relationships fail... | Esther Perel.* YouTube. www.youtube.com/watch?v=QRpV9K11K3M.

Iacoboni, M. (2008). *Mirroring people: The new science of how we connect with others.* Farrar, Straus and Giroux.

Johnson, S. (2008). *Hold me tight: Seven conversations for a lifetime of love.* Little, Brown and Company.

Jung, C. G. (1980). Psychology and Alchemy, *Collected works of C. G. Jung,* Volume 12. Princeton University Press.

Kabat-Zinn, J. (1990). *Full catastrophe living: Using the wisdom of your body and mind to face stress, pain, and illness.* Random House.

Kleinplatz, P., & Menard, A. (2020). *Magnificent sex: Lessons from extraordinary lovers.* Routledge.

Laitman, M. (2013). *Connected by nature's law.* ARI.

Machin, A. (2022). *Why we love: The new science behind our closest relationships.* Pegasus Books Ltd.

Maslow, A. (1998). *Toward a psychology of being.* Wiley.

McCarthy, B. (2014). *Rekindling desire.* Routledge.

Mellody, P. (1989). *Facing codependence: What it is, where it comes from, how it sabotages our lives.* Harper & Row.

Nagoski, E. (2015). *Come as you are: The surprising new science that will transform your sex life.* Simon & Schuster Paperbacks.

Norwood, R. (1985). *Women who love too much: When you keep wishing and hoping he'll change.* Pocket Books.

Peck, S. (1978). *The road less traveled: A new psychology of love, traditional values and spiritual growth.* Simon & Schuster.

Perel, E. (2006). *Mating in captivity: Unlocking erotic intelligence.* HarperCollins Publishers.

Pinkola Estés, C. (1997). *Women who run with the wolves: Myths and stories of the wild woman archetype.* Ballantine Books.

Pueblo, Y. (2018). *Inward*. Andrews McMeel Publishing.

Real, T. (1997). *I don't want to talk about it: Overcoming the secret legacy of male depression*. Simon & Schuster.

Real, T. (2007). *The new rules of marriage: What you need to know to make love work*. Ballantine Books.

Real, T. (2022). *Us: Getting past you and me to build a more loving relationship*. Rodale Books.

Rohr, R. and Lamott, A. (2021). *Breathing under water: Spirituality and the twelve steps*. Franciscan Media.

Rosenberg, M. (2015). *Nonviolent communication: A language of life*. Puddledancer Press.

Rowling, J. K. (2000). *Harry potter and the goblet of fire*. Scholastic.

Schwartz, R. C. & Sweezy, M. (2019). *Internal family systems therapy*. 2nd ed. Guilford Publications.

Siegel, D. J. (2017). *Mind: A journey to the heart of being human*. W. W. Norton & Company, Inc.

Thibaut, J. & Kelley, H. (1959). *The social psychology of groups*. John Wiley & Sons.

Thibaut, J. & Kelley, H. (1978). *Interpersonal relations: A theory of interdependence*. John Wiley & Sons.

Walster, E., Walster, G. W., & Berscheid, E. (1978). *Equity: Theory and research*. Allyn and Bacon.

Webb, J. (2012). *Running on empty: Overcome your childhood emotional neglect*. Morgan James Publishing.

Weiner-Davis, M. (2002). *The divorce remedy: The proven 7-step program for saving your marriage*. P 54. Simon & Schuster.

Winch, R. (1958). *Mate-Selection: A study of complementary needs.* Harper & Brothers.

Woolf, V. (1931). *The Waves.* Hogarth Press.

Printed in the USA
CPSIA information can be obtained
at www.ICGtesting.com
LVHW091547310324
775972LV00002B/283